DREAMING OF A DIVINE LIFE

DREAMING OF A DIVINE LIFE

One Woman Remembers Her
Truth That May Awaken Us All!

Joanne Lee Philpot

Copyright © 2017 Joanne Lee Philpot

The moral right of the author has been asserted.

Apart from any fair dealing for the purposes of research or private study, or criticism or review, as permitted under the Copyright, Designs and Patents Act 1988, this publication may only be reproduced, stored or transmitted, in any form or by any means, with the prior permission in writing of the publishers, or in the case of reprographic reproduction in accordance with the terms of licences issued by the Copyright Licensing Agency. Enquiries concerning reproduction outside those terms should be sent to the publishers.

Matador
9 Priory Business Park,
Wistow Road, Kibworth Beauchamp,
Leicestershire. LE8 0RX
Tel: 0116 279 2299
Email: books@troubador.co.uk
Web: www.troubador.co.uk/matador
Twitter: @matadorbooks

ISBN 978 1788035 088

British Library Cataloguing in Publication Data.
A catalogue record for this book is available from the British Library.

Printed and bound by CPI Group (UK) Ltd, Croydon, CR0 4YY
Typeset in 11pt Aldine by Troubador Publishing Ltd, Leicester, UK

Matador is an imprint of Troubador Publishing Ltd

Dedicated to all of us searchers and seekers of Love, Freedom, Truth and Joy and to my four children who teach and awaken me every day!

CONTENTS

Preface: YOU ARE LOVE	ix
Chapter 1: Dreaming of Leaving	1
Chapter 2: Buying the Perfect Yoga Retreat	23
Chapter 3: The Dream Goes Wrong	43
Chapter 4: Harvesting and Meeting My Guru	64
Chapter 5: A Lucky Escape and Our Chakras	84
Chapter 6: Releasing Our Fears	103
Chapter 7: My Yogic Diet	122
Chapter 8: The Meaning of Love	143
Chapter 9: The Laws of Karma, Attraction and Love	164
Chapter 10: Our Children are Our Heroes	186
Chapter 11: Connecting with My Divine Self	205
Chapter 12: Remembering My Truth	226
Chapter 13: Salvation	247
Chapter 14: Peace, Love, Unity and Equality	269
Epilogue: Eternal Truths and Secrets to Living a Divine Life	293
Bibliography	297

PREFACE
YOU ARE LOVE

There is only Love! And God is the Divine Love that lives in every heart and soul. The entire universe has been created by love, for it's the energy that keeps it evolving and it whispers to you; if only you can stop talking, quieten your mind and begin to listen.

When you fall in love, you are given a glorious awakening of the 'Divinity' within your beloved and you think it is special because your 'True Loving Self' has been hidden by the false fearful ego – this is a compelling spiritual experience which opens your heart. When you are hurt by love or go through challenging situations, this heightens your awareness and transforms your negative mind, allowing Love Energy to flow through you into this world which awakens all beings and brings peace to us all!

For 'You Are Love'; this is your most sublime feeling and your ultimate truth, as it never wants or needs anything, it only gives, heals and makes you whole. This love is our spiritual connection with each other, all living beings and the source of creation that we have all forgotten. It's our sacredness with life that we must feel again and it's the lover, beloved and God becoming one. Therefore let us not remember our hurts, sufferings or mistakes of the past, but let us be present and, in the miracle of now, begin again, forgiving each other and uniting our hearts, our minds and our souls forever in Love!

This book is my story, my journey and the self-realisation of how I came to remember this Eternal Truth! I believe it will help you to feel the 'Love Within You' and may it assist you in living a 'Divine Life'.

JOANNE LEE PHILPOT

CHAPTER 1

DREAMING OF LEAVING

Each and every one of us has the magic power to transform our lives and our world. Each and every one of us can Dream and make our Dreams come true.

JOANNE LEE PHILPOT

Everybody needs a dream and my dream has always been to create a yoga retreat somewhere warm and peaceful by the sea. I'd been teaching yoga in England for many years in various gyms and health clubs, but I wanted to teach in an environment where people could relax, learn about yoga and meditation, and enjoy delicious food. They would meet a Himalayan Guru, be taught eternal truths and secrets to life and have a realisation that they are Divine Loving Beings!

My handsome Italian partner was convinced of my dream too and said it would be great for us to go on an adventure with our three young daughters. We thought Italy was the place for our retreat as Italy has 'La Dolce

Vita' – the 'sweet life' – with the delightful food, history and delightful medieval castle towns.

My partner grew up in Naples in southern Italy and in his twenties he went to live in London where I met him in a fashionable, stylish nightclub. He was the charming, sexy guy behind the bar and I was the gorgeous girl with the long blonde hair. Our eyes met and we fell in love! We were such a dynamic couple, the life and soul of every party, and a pair of 'free spirits'. I remember when we first started dating he called me up at nine thirty one morning telling me to meet him at a café in Soho. When I arrived there he was sitting outside drinking tequila, and had been awake and partying all night long! He poured me a drink, shouted for the music to begin and took my hand, leading me out into the middle of the street where we began dancing. My long, pink skirt twirled around my legs as we danced and lost ourselves in each other's eyes, completely oblivious to all the people staring at us as they walked to work. We were causing quite a sensation with people hanging out of their office windows clapping and cheering us on!

Three months later I became pregnant and my partner took me to Italy to meet his family. First we went to Milan where I was welcomed by his extremely caring papa who cooked us up the most delicious southern Italian food and by his step-mamma, brother, sister and cousins. Next we jumped on a train to Florence to see the statue of *David* by Michelangelo and travelled down to Naples where we visited Pompeii to walk through its incredible streets and explore its ancient villas. We then drove along the dangerous yet breathtaking coastal road to the pretty town of Sorrento where I was introduced to my partner's vivacious Italian mamma and on to the stunning towns of Positano and Amalfi that were precariously built into the steep hillsides. Over the next few years, as our other children were born, we went on holiday and stayed with my partner's family many times. They were happy that we had decided to move to Italy and said they would help us out when we arrived.

My parents were also ready for a change in life. They had a little shop in our home town of Leigh-on-Sea, Essex called 'Day Dream Designs' which sold contemporary, handmade metal furniture. My mum, who is very creative, drew the designs and my dad who is brilliant with his hands made them and we thought maybe they could set up a shop in Italy. We put both our bungalows up for sale and with the combined profits we hoped we would be able to buy two houses on the same plot of land, not too far from the sea and have further accommodation for ten guests at our yoga retreat. While waiting for potential buyers my parents and I searched the internet for all the romantic Italian properties, fantasising about what the retreat would look like and willing our dream to come true!

Throughout my life I have always felt an enthralling spiritual calling which has never ceased! When I was young I craved knowledge, wisdom and meaning to life's deeper questions and its mysteries. I believed in a higher power, yet I was endlessly searching for something to fill the emptiness I sensed within. I travelled to many New Age festivals and sacred sites all over England where I played the drums, danced around fires, and had enlightening talks with other truth seekers all night long. I read the Tarot cards for all my friends, practised a few Wiccan rituals and knew there was a magical, spiritual side to life other than just surviving or the accumulation of money and material things! I wanted to truly live and experience it all, so I could awaken myself to the truth and be it all! For the more awakened we become, the more our energy changes inside and we give spiritually kinder vibrations outside which changes our lives, changes other people's lives and ultimately changes the world!

During my teenage years I worked as a model and travelled to many different countries. Travelling was the best education of my life, living on my own, getting an insight into other cultures and going through many joyful and painful life lessons. I was young, beautiful, wild and impulsive, and I had a pure heart and was always sincere. But I seemed to have a constant struggle between my kind, giving nature and my selfish taking nature. I tried to escape my struggles and fill the emptiness inside by experimenting with drugs and alcohol. They expanded my mind and enhanced my personality for a while, yet allowed me to be used by others which left me feeling lost and frustrated. I had a normal loving childhood and my parents gave me everything they could afford.

However their beliefs that success is measured by how much money you have which had been conditioned into them from their parents, grandparents and our society affected me. I focused all my energy into chasing cash, becoming materialistic and confused, and perhaps saying yes to people and to negative situations when really

I should have been saying no. I didn't have much self-respect or self-love back then and consequently I gave myself away at times, having rich boyfriends, becoming a high-class escort and flying around the world in private planes!

I remember travelling first class to Hong Kong when I was about eighteen to be the companion of a Saudi prince and telling my parents I was on a 'modelling' job. The decadence of the exclusive hotel I stayed in with its enticing all-inclusive room service excited me and dressing up in a red Chinese dress to have dinner at the Jumbo floating restaurant in the harbour was thrilling. Although the prince was a wealthy man, he was a lost soul and would get very drunk, laying his head in my lap and crying that nobody loved him; I stroked his expensive hair-transplanted head and tried to comfort him!

Yet even then my spiritual callings were a lot stronger than my material desires as the next day, all alone, I jumped on a boat to Lantau Island and then onto a crowded bus with lots of monks and pilgrims to drive on a winding road, up the side of a mountain and in the heat of the midday sunshine, walk up four hundred steps to breathlessly stand before the Tian Tan, which is the biggest Buddha in the world. It was one of the most awe-inspiring sights and overwhelming feelings that I have ever experienced and it gave me such a transcendent connection with the higher power within us all that it brought tears of joy and gratitude to my eyes.

Coming through customs at Heathrow Airport I had to conceal the bejewelled bracelet and enormous wad of money that the prince had given me and quickly jumped into a taxi all the way to my parents' house. I told them that while I was in Hong Kong I met a man and we went to the casino to play roulette. I then took the money out of my handbag and to make it more dramatic I threw it up in the air, simultaneously exclaiming that I'd won! As £40,000 gently floated to the living room carpet I stuck my arm out to show them the dazzling real diamond bracelet and the look of incredulous amazement on both their faces was priceless – because things like that never happened to working-class girls born in East London! My parents then helped me to invest the money into a pretty flat in North London.

During my brief time as an escort I had lots of amusing experiences and, of course, some not quite so pleasant. At times I felt unworthy, and my belief in a higher power weakened. I ended up in many precarious circumstances, yet somehow I always came through unscathed and had amazing insights into life! For I adored all the drama and all the chaos, and I didn't condemn any experience because I knew they would help me develop myself further and eventually lead me to choose infinitely better ones! As the nature of life is change and evolution, if I wanted to change and evolve I had to embrace all types of experiences, both positive and negative, and see the wisdom and love in them all. Anyway, how could I have the good things in life if I had never gone through the bad? How could I have success if I had never tried or failed and how could I feel love if I had never felt fear or hate? All of us have come from the oneness and light of heaven which is the spiritual world, to experience the separation and darkness on earth so we would yearn for and create that oneness and light again.

My callings led me to seek out alternative book shops and to devour as many books as I could find on spiritual teachings and the meaning of life. I have always been a bookworm and books have been like milestones, waiting to be read and giving me deep realisations when the time was right. I was drawn to many different types of philosophy, spirituality and theology, reading lots of books on Buddhism, Paganism, the Native American Indians, and on yoga where I began practising the asanas (postures) in my bedroom. I learnt from the Buddhists that compassion is the most important quality to cultivate and we may cultivate it by putting our attention on the most caring person we know, thinking about how kind and forgiving they have been to us, then transferring these feelings to our parents, relatives, friends and eventually to all beings we come into contact with.

I would often think to myself, *am I being truly compassionate to include others or is my compassion only towards my family and friends?* I realised that I must open my heart and transform my mind, developing tolerance, acceptance and compassion towards all beings which brings me happiness! I understood how important it was that I stopped judging and criticising people and not to think about others in a jealous, hurtful way because this was my ego wanting to be superior over them which causes discontent in the world. When this selfish behaviour arose in me, I knew I had more negativity to let go of and more love to cultivate within; also it made me understand that I did not want to behave like that again. When I saw this behaviour in others I felt it was just wounded reactions and an unconscious asking for peace, love and help. Therefore I needed to stay calm and try not to react negatively, but see the best in people and have positive thoughts and feelings towards them. For the more we help others, the more we help ourselves and being of service to people is spiritual practice that heightens the collective consciousness of us all!

In my early twenties I rented out my flat in London and travelled to India. Walking through the hot, busy streets I was amazed at some of the people offering you their breakfast at the side of the dusty road. The poverty was all around me, but I was totally captivated by the incredible colours, aromatic smells and mystical rituals of Indian life. I then lived in Australia for seven years where I attended meditation meetings, learnt about different religions and had lots of interesting experiences, such as posing for calendars and working as a dancer in the first-ever 'Table Dancing Club of Australia!' The owners put my photo on an enormous billboard and on opening night the club was packed with Australia's male VIPs. It was all very tasteful and only topless which I didn't mind as I was a free spirit and used to going to nudist beaches. Coming off stage I could barely walk as both my garters were stuffed full of money; I remember making around $5,000 in one week! It was empowering working as a table dancer twenty-two years ago and it gave me lots of self-esteem and confidence with men, which I needed because even though I had a wild side, underneath I was a nice, shy, quiet girl!

I also had some challenging experiences while in

Australia such as being arrested for 'one million dollars of marijuana' which my boyfriend at the time had been secretly growing in allotments and hiding in an enormous shed outside the back of our rented house. The next-door neighbour became suspicious and called the police, and, as I was the only person in the house, they arrested me and locked me up in a dirty, smelly cell at the police station for three nights. I remember feeling tremendously scared and claustrophobic, and began crying and pressing the buzzer on the wall, desperately wanting to be let out. However, after an hour or so, my tears subsided and I felt calm and resilient. I looked up towards the heavens and implored, "You can lock away my physical body but never my spiritual soul which is eternally free!" I was then spiritually guided to find a solicitor who actually wanted to help people. He got me released on bail and thankfully proved my innocence with the whole story coming out in the newspapers and appearing on the evening news!

Yet I always tried to learn from my experiences and never allowed my heart to become hardened by them and kept my optimistic, open-minded outlook on life. As I felt each and every one of us needs to experience the negative things in this world so that we can begin to want and ask the Universe-Spirit-God for the positive improvements in our ever-evolving lives!

I knew then I was on my 'spiritual journey' and that I was turning into a 'modern hippy' because all I wanted to do was awaken all people and save the world!

My travels and challenges ignited the passion in my heart and assisted me on my path of self-discovery. They were opening my eyes to see life on this magnificent planet as a continual search for meaning, realising that every experience has the potential to help me see the truth within all things. The Native American Indians tell us that we each perceive the world around us differently and everything depends on how we individually see it, as the same object or event may appear fearful to some people, loving to others or completely uninteresting to the rest. Therefore everything is relative according to the reality that we perceive and life is either good or bad according to the 'state of mind' in which we look at it; thus it's valuable to honour the truth as it is seen from every being's sacred point of view.

When I returned to London I went to see the Dalai Lama at the Royal Albert Hall where he gave a stupendous talk which influenced me profoundly, inspiring me to take on the revered practice of thinking more about others and wanting to ease their pain and suffering. Subsequently I began feeling an even stronger calling, yearning and longing for spiritual fulfilment, for the secrets to life and the search for God. I seemed to always be helping others and remember my dad telling me once, "Joanne, you must stop trying to save the world, you must look after yourself," but I didn't understand who my true self was back then – I just wanted to give peace and love to all, as I knew that love is strength! Love is stronger than fear or any negative thought or feeling that divides us and makes us feel bad. Love is the combination of every emotion that we have ever felt and it brings us all together and makes us feel good. We just have to be brave enough to love ourselves

and give love out to each other for:
"Love is the sacred medicine that we have all forgotten!"

At that time I attended my first yoga class and became completely fascinated by yoga, and spiritually guided to study a course to become a Hatha yoga teacher. During the first year of the course, my teacher taught me that yoga is the science of life and a complete system of self-development which is based on the evolution of human consciousness. I studied yogic psychology and philosophy, writing papers on the ancient scriptures of Hinduism and Buddhism, and on the Vedic Sutras. The word 'Sutra' means 'thread' in the Sanskrit language, which is the oldest language in the world and the language of yoga. Sutras are threads of sacred words and knowledge that have been passed down by the self-realised beings, the Ancient Yogis. These teachings promote ethical principles of non-violence, truth and purity and moral disciplines of non-attachment and self-study for us to live by. They instruct us to transform our negative, chaotic minds into positive, peaceful minds by cultivating the spiritual values of love, forgiveness, generosity and contentment.

The Ancient Yogis have given us eternal truths and secrets to life. They teach us to be in harmony with nature and to live by the divine laws of the universe that maintain the life and evolution of all things. I learnt about the yogic law of cause and effect – karma, which states that every action has a reaction and that the act of giving will always initiate its opposite reaction of receiving. Thus, if we want to receive love we must give out love, if we want to feel joy we must make others feel joy and if we want kindness and honesty from people we must be kind and honest to them. Once we bestow these values on others it spreads virtue throughout the entire universe and consequently we receive back all that we give.

As the months went by during the days alone in my North London flat, I read the sacred books I needed to pass my course and I practised yoga asanas and silenced my mind in meditation. At night I dressed up in glamour dresses, putting on high heels and lots of make-up to work as a table dancer in the West End clubs so I could pay my mortgage. Yet I was beginning to change! Yoga was bringing up deep-seated feelings and releasing repressed emotions from within me. I cried easily because I didn't want to feel alone, materialistic or empty any more. I wanted meaning to my life! I wanted a sense of fulfilment, I wanted community, and I yearned for that connection that we are all yearning for – the Connection with Spirit and Oneness with the Source of Creation!

As I immersed my being with the ancient wisdom of the sacred books, I found one message repeatedly told through them all: *that we are already one with the Source of Creation* which is the collective consciousness of every soul in the universe and which I call Spirit, God or the Divine. When woman and man first existed upon the earth they were equals and lived in happiness, but then we lost our light and fear and greed came into being which created two separate natures; the ego personality which is the lower physical nature that takes, and the true self which is our higher divine nature that gives.

Thus in this world of duality we alternate between our two natures which causes unhappiness, suffering and separation from the oneness and true higher self within.

Yoga in Sanskrit means union! Yoga is a spiritual discipline which raises our awareness, bringing mind, body and spirit/soul into alignment and giving us self-realisation which is the union of our true self – our soul consciousness with Universal God Consciousness. Self-realisation is our natural, joyful state of being; it means to live in the present moment and to be a loving, calm person who is free from anger, worry and negativity. Enlightenment means the same thing; letting the light in heals our negative mind so we see the light of Spirit which is the same light within all living beings! Self-realisation is not about being special, admired or exalted; it's about being thankful, humble and helping others.

"For we are already enlightened, we just don't realise it!"

Yoga gives us joy and peace and the purpose of life is the expansion of joy and peace for all! For me it does not matter if a person is religious or not; what matters is that they are a caring human being who is aware and respectful of other people's feelings and different points of view. All people want to be happy, have good health, love and abundance, and I believe the basic nature of humanity is kind, honourable and compassionate. I feel we all yearn for a safe society and personal fulfilment, and that deep within we all sense frustration at living in such a selfish acquisitive world that we try to escape it by filling our lives with material distractions! Yet I was beginning to learn that success is not measured by how much money we have or by how big our house is or by what car we drive; true success is measured by how much joy we feel, by how much joy we have given others and by how much we can change this world for the better; this is true wealth.

During the second year of my teacher training, while living on my own with two cats for company, my negative, taking ego seemed to be getting the better of me. I was caught between being a 'good' holy yogini (female yogi) and being what I thought was a 'bad' unholy person who had done immoral things, thought she was never good enough and wanted to try all the tempting pleasures our materialistic society has in it. For I was mixing with the wrong negative people, I was still occasionally taking drugs and alcohol and I had no self-discipline in my life. One morning I woke up not wanting to go to my yoga course because I'd spent the previous night out on the town partying and I felt awful. I called up my teacher and lied to her saying I hurt my ankle, but she must have sensed something in my voice because she became very firm with me. "Joanne," she commanded, "you will make an amazing yoga teacher one day and I know you will help many people in the future. You must come to class now and finish this course!"

Her words awakened me to the way I was living my life. I knew I had to overcome my lower nature and start believing in myself and soon yoga and my spiritual lifestyle became more important to me than going out partying all night long.

Subsequently I started reading more books from spiritual masters all over the world and again their messages were telling me the same secrets and truths as the Ancient Yogis: *'that we all think too much and each thought we think is based in either love, which brings us pleasure, or fear, which brings us pain.* Negative fear-based thoughts of anger, resentment or worry create stress in the mind and disconnect us from Spirit. This blocks the flow of Life-Force Energy called prana which disrupts bodily functions, damages our cells and contributes to actions that may be harmful to others. In yoga we learn to think and feel with positive love-based thoughts and feelings of goodness, truthfulness and gentleness that bring harmony to the mind and reconnect us to Spirit. This frees the flow of prana which rejuvenates the entire body and contributes to actions that aid others' wellbeing.

For our eternal soul, which is the combined awareness that we all share within, talks to us through our inspiring thoughts, feelings and experiences. Our feelings awaken us, they are our 'inner guidance' and they tell us the truth because, if something is good for us, we feel happy and if something is bad for us, we feel sad.

It is natural to feel fear and to react negatively which is caused by the unfulfilled desires of our selfish taking nature and by the outdated beliefs of our society because we have all been wrongly programmed and addicted to automatically think, feel and react in this undesirable way for a very long time! Fear-based emotions stop us from living joyful lives. If we believe everything around us is always negative and the world is a frightening, awful place with everyone out to get us, we react in the same way back to others which causes more pain and anguish; this is deluded thinking and only the fear in our egoic minds. Planet Earth is our safe, abundant, beautiful home and it's a place of peace, love and freedom – if we choose to perceive it this way.

In the last year of my yoga course I fell madly in love with my engaging Italian partner. We had attracted each other at the right time of our lives and because of our lack of self-love we had both been taken advantage of by others – thus we tried to heal one another. My partner moved into my flat but became jealous of me working as a table dancer and we argued about it constantly. One night while I was working, I gazed around at the artificially created pleasure dome of the high-class men's club and had an astounding realisation! I felt the negative energy and lustful testosterone oppressively hanging in the air; I felt the other girls' loneliness and utter desperateness of their self-created situations and I saw the way they were treated as a lower commodity and how money had become their God. The reality of my delusion hit me straight in the heart! *What am I doing here?* I pleaded to myself. *I don't want to do this any more; I want to be a yogini!*

The insight and humiliation was unbearable. I pushed past the aroused sweaty men, grabbed my bag and ran out of the club into the cold night air with black make-up tears streaking my cheeks. I rummaged frantically inside my bag for change and found a phone box to call up my partner. He said he didn't want me to work there again and reassured me that he would help pay the mortgage so I wouldn't have to take my clothes off for money any longer!

Shortly after, at thirty years old, I became pregnant and an inner harmony arose inside me for the first time. At my yoga course, I would stand on my head, meditate and chant sacred songs with my fellow students who told me what a spiritual baby I would have (which turned out to be true). I attended a wonderful yoga for pregnancy class close to where I lived and it was so empowering to be around twenty pregnant women all helping each other get into the asanas, practising our breathing, birthing positions and massaging each other's backs. After giving birth, the ladies would bring their gorgeous newborns into class for everyone to see and it was extremely encouraging to listen to their birthing experiences. The night I had my baby I remember the nurse told me to put her in the cot to sleep, but I just couldn't let her go! As I breastfed her I looked deep into her eyes telling her through my tears of thankfulness, how much she will be loved, how protected she will be and how she will help others and make a difference in this world.

The profound effect of having my baby and of yoga coming into my life reinforced my belief in the higher power of God once again! Not as a man with a white beard, but as the Pure Collective Consciousness which we are all a part of and as the Pure Positive Peace and Divine Love Energy that we all have inside. I felt that God had been depicted in a fearful, vengeful, yet loving way which has had confusing consequences on how we conditionally love each other and on what we think is right and wrong. I understood that hell and the devil do not exist. They only exist within the illusion of our relative ego mind as fear, doubt, worry and separation from love, and that there is no judgement or condemnation in life, only the consequences and results of our own positive or negative thoughts, feelings, words and actions. I knew I had to pay attention to what the enlightened ones tell us; that there is only *Love in Creation*! Love is unity, it frees and heals us; it's our correct feelings of innocence, worthiness and happiness, and our true higher nature. Fear is separation, it withholds and causes illness, it's our incorrect feelings of guilt, unworthiness and unhappiness, and our false lower nature. We will constantly swing between these two emotions and variations of them until we take on the responsibility to choose love over fear, truth over delusion, knowledge over ignorance and God over Ego in every moment.

At the end of my teacher training and once I had passed my exams, a yogi friend asked me to take over his class at a school in Soho. It was the first yoga class I had ever taught and I remember all the students looking at me expectantly. I felt self-conscious and nervous, yet during the hour-and-a-half session I sensed a serene otherworldly presence all around me that was guiding my words and actions. The more classes I taught the more confident I became and, due to all the teaching, studying and yoga and meditation I was doing, I began having a shift in consciousness! This change of perception instigated an even deeper feeling of empathy towards nature, animals, and other people and most importantly towards me. I realised that I had to accept my past and accept myself so I could become the person I had always dreamed of – so I could be the true yoga teacher I had envisioned because;

"Acceptance is the pathway to peace!"

When we are peaceful, compassionate and feeling good, we vibrate love out to all people and wellness through our whole body. Therefore let us all try to be happy for those people who have found happiness, be caring towards those who are unhappy and for the people who are wicked and evil, well, let's look at them with indifference not hatred as they may have never known compassion or tenderness. They may have never had a family nor any friends, and they may feel hurt, wounded and unworthy of love which makes them react in a hateful way towards others. Yet eventually through their own choices and experiences, they will one day become awakened, evolving towards the Divine to be helpers of humanity!

Once we heal the separation between ourselves by changing and transforming our fear, selfishness and negativity; once we hold in the highest regard all living beings and our natural environment; once we raise our awareness and enhance ourselves further, only then will we remember the truth within our hearts, minds and souls, and allow this goodness to flow through us which *evolves all life and awakens us all!*

"This is the beginning of our New Love Awareness,
Of our New Consciousness of the Heart,
And it's emerging throughout the world at this time"

I learnt a great deal from all of my adventures when I was younger and on a deeper level I know they definitely affected me. However I do not regret any of them because everything I went through, every lesson I chose, guided and prepared me for the spiritual path of yoga; it was predestined by my soul for my greater good and all part of my awakening.

I felt fortunate and spiritually guided to have been given eternal truths and secrets to life, yet even though I had studied so many scriptures and books I was not putting into practice or really living all I had learnt. For my mind was still full of negativity, my reactions were not truly loving and my heart was not wholly compassionate. Furthermore, even though I understood the meaning of God as a concept, I needed to experience the 'feeling of God, the feeling of Love' which every soul yearns for – even though they may not realise it! Having young children and being in a demanding relationship, it was difficult to find the time and a peaceful place to quieten my mind and open my heart. I thought that moving to Italy and creating a yoga retreat would give me self-realisation and a 'Divine Life!'

Subsequently my family and I travelled to Italy many times trying to find the region we wanted to live in. We searched for different locations on the internet until we finally found the most glorious place with thousands of palm trees along sandy beaches, in San Benedetto del Tronto, southern Le Marche on the Adriatic coast called the 'Riviera delle Palme'. It had very stylish shops, many inviting beach restaurants and there were lots of medieval castle towns in the area. San Benedetto was three and a half hours by car over the mountains to Rome, where we dreamed of having lunch by the famous Trevi Fountain and exploring the ancient Colosseum. We all agreed this was the place for us, but unfortunately we didn't travel there beforehand to check things out.

At that time the property market in England was good and we sold both our bungalows within a month of each other. My parents bought a caravan for the journey down to Italy which was packed full with their worldly possessions, having put all the large furniture in storage. They towed it around to our house with their two cats and dog inside, looking tired and a little in shock as they were now homeless and parked on our driveway! They stayed two nights, getting ready with all the maps before heading off to the middle of Italy – what an experience for them. I really admire my parents at the age of sixty jumping into the unknown and going on the biggest adventure of their lives. How brave they were! Off they drove through France and the Swiss Alps to eventually arrive at Led Zeppelin campsite which was our meeting point in Le Marche, Italy.

Meanwhile, back in England, I packed our personal possessions into our car and my brother and yogi friend drove it down to Italy with my big dog and spiritual cat in the back. Then my partner and I with our three young daughters Lola, six years old, Gina, three years old and my little baby Sienna, six months old, said sad goodbyes to our family, friends and to my beloved grandmother who was upset to see us go. As we boarded the plane we were excited and toasted the start of our new, exciting life together with a glass of champagne!

Arriving at Ancona Airport, my dad picked us up and we drove to the campsite which was similar to Butlin's (British holiday camps) but Italian-style. We rented a chalet onsite and, as it was September, we sunbathed on the beautiful beaches every day and dined out and explored the area in the evenings. Friday and Saturday nights at the campsite were party nights with my children singing and dancing on stage to the awful Italian music!

"We had arrived"

CHAPTER 2

BUYING THE PERFECT YOGA RETREAT

*I am in the process of creating my new life.
I am living in the moment with my True Self.
I am changing my negative thoughts and releasing my outdated
beliefs. I am in control of what I think, say and do therefore I
choose Love over Fear and positive thoughts that make me
'Feel Good.' For I am a Divine Loving Being
I am limitless and I am creating my own Destiny!*

JOANNE LEE PHILPOT

My family and I left the campsite in a convoy of two cars and a caravan. We had rented two apartments backing onto each other in part of a lovely 300-year-old stone house with traditional vaulted ceilings that was high on the hill of a medieval town called Acquaviva Picena and ten meandering minutes' drive to the beaches of San Benedetto del Tronto. Our landlord was a jolly Italian man who was often tipsy from his superb homemade red wine and sometimes had secret liaisons with his mistress in the upstairs apartment while his wife was at home two hours away!

The view from the house was a panoramic feast for the eyes, all the way down to the blue Adriatic Sea. In the mornings with the spectacular red sun coming up over the horizon and the children sleeping, I took my mat and practised yoga and meditation. I began as always by relaxing, then with Salute to the Sun which consists of twelve asanas that kept my body supple and youthful. I believe that with the Spiritual Life-Force Energy of the Sun flowing so strongly through me, it was heightening my awareness and giving me deep revelations! In those inspiring moments I felt energised, peaceful and in harmony with all things. For I had been given a brief taste of the perfect state of yoga and I wanted to stay in that Divine place forever!

My Sat Guru (Sat means true) Yogiraj Siddhanath describes yoga in his wonderful book *Wings to Freedom, Mystic Revelations from Babaji and the Himalayan Yogis*:

> *"Yoga is the science of all sciences because it deals with the very essence of the evolution and wellbeing of humanity. It is the one and only science offering the knowledge and practice of total transformation from Man the Brute, to Man the Man, to Man the God. It is for this reason that the Supreme Love, the Love for the Divine and Love for Humanity may be experienced through Yoga!"*

We then had to prove that we lived in Italy by acquiring our residency at the local town hall. All of us, including the children, drove through the high castle walls that encircled the tiny historical centre and walked into the delightfully decorated building which was covered in hand-painted frescoes. It took a long time to fill in and sign all the paperwork, but as we walked outside into the glorious sunshine we all felt proud to have our precious Italian identity cards in our hands.

Next we called up lots of estate agents and began looking at properties, searching for our dream yoga retreat. What we needed were two houses with further accommodation for ten yoga guests on a small plot of land and not too far from the sea. I found the Italian estate agents eager to help, yet they didn't seem to have that much experience of real estate. They drove you miles into the countryside showing you lots of brick ruins and three-roomed huts that were extremely overpriced, and told you to use your imagination as they presumed you had millions in the bank because you were English! We viewed one property which we thought we could renovate into our retreat; however, when we got home we found out it had miraculously gone up €100,000!

Eventually we did find a property 8kms from the seaside town of Cupra Marittima and 3kms from a sixteenth-century, medieval castle town called Ripatransone. This mini-hilltop city is surrounded by the most attractive countryside which on one side has the highest view all the way down to the sea and on the other has the incredible view of the Gran Sasso and Sibillini mountains which run through the middle of Italy. The old historical centre is encased by high Roman turreted walls kept in perfect condition and, when I first walked through this little town which boasts the narrowest alleyway in Italy, I was in complete awe as I had never seen anything so quaint and charming! My first impression was of a picture-perfect postcard as almost all the houses are built of old exposed brickwork with romantic Romeo and Juliet balconies and, of course, the white washing flapping in the wind!

As I strolled through the dusty, cobbled streets with the bells of one of the thirteen churches ringing in my ears, I felt taken back to another time where horses and carts were the fast cars of today. I came across the local gelateria (ice cream parlour) in a beautiful arched, vaulted walkway that made the most delicious homemade ice creams and, walking further down the old cobblestone hill, gazed in amazement at the impressive duomo (cathedral) and its spectacular gold-domed roof. I then took a seat outside the local bar in the warm sun to experience the most marvellous macchiato coffee and I knew this bar would become a firm favourite with my children as they made on the premises the most sumptuous little cakes I had ever tasted!

The property we found consisted of the main house with living accommodation on the first floor and animal pens and wine vats on the ground floor. There was also planning permission to knock down the large barn outside and build our second house. The main house had lots of extra rooms with separate entrances that could be used for our yoga guests and there was 4,000 m^2 of land surrounded by vegetable fields and green forests with the most spectacular view all the way down the valley to the sparkling sea which was ten minutes away by car. The girls' school was a short drive up the hill past the picturesque Monastero Passioniste (the local monastery) and on the way you could see the magnificent snow-capped mountains that seemed to go on forever; gazing at that view would give me much needed hope and inspiration through the months to come.

My partner's step-papa had a small building company in Naples and he drove over to check the house out before we purchased it. He gave us quotes to reconstruct the main house and take down the barn to build the second house. We were happy with the quotes he gave us and asked him to be our builder as we had enough money to proceed in buying and renovating the property.

At the Italian solicitor's office, all the people who own the house have to be present, in this case four older women, including a farmer's wife who cried through the whole proceedings because she was selling off the old family home! We had an English interpreter who charged a fortune, but just as we were about to sign all the documents we realised my partner had not been included on the deeds of the house because he had not attended an important meeting! He became angry and started shouting at everyone then stormed out of the office leaving the Italian ladies sitting in astonishment. I ran after him, trying to calm his wounded ego down and persuaded him to come back inside and sort it out. Eventually we decided to split the property four ways, making sure that my parents, who were putting in a lot more euros, received their money back when it was sold.

When Christmas Day arrived my partner was still

brooding over what had happened at the solicitors and during Christmas dinner an argument erupted between him and my dad, and it was dreadful as they were yelling at each other in front of the children! If there was one thing my partner needed to do in life, it was to control his anger. Anger is a natural feeling that allows us to say no to the things we do not like. Underneath anger is always fear and attachment to the things in this world and underneath fear and attachment is always longing for peace, love and understanding. When anger is uncontrolled because of wrong thinking and living in the past or future it can become abusive and harmful to others.

Buddha said:

"We are shaped by our thoughts. The secret to the health of both mind and body is not to mourn for the past, worry about the future or anticipate troubles, but to live in the present moment wisely and earnestly."

Through my studies I have found that all the power of the universe is in the here and now because fear does not exist in the present and because only this Divine Moment exists! When we align with the timeless now, there are no bad memories or past conditionings, all is forgiven and we are free to begin again with new thoughts and new feelings. Being present means concentrating on what we are doing in this moment; to be mindful and aware of every action and not thinking of other things in the past or future. God which is love only works in present time so we need to be present and feel the peace, feel the love by listening to the truthful teachings and inner guidance of our soul and heart, not the incorrect thoughts and cravings of the ego mind. For Ego-Fear always seeks to separate us and wants us to take things seriously while Spirit-Love always seeks to unite us and wants us to see the soulful, happy side of life.

After Christmas, my partner and I were packing up our belongings in the apartment to move into our new house and I could feel the tension between us. We began arguing then shouting at each other with him swearing, threatening and verbally abusing me. He yelled that he'd had enough of me and my parents and was going to drive to his father's house in Milan because our relationship was over… I couldn't believe he was leaving; before in England I would have gone mad at him and tried to stop him, but I just let him go. As he left in the car I began to see the many things that were wrong in my relationship and the many things that were wrong with *me*!

I felt extremely lonely and unfulfilled and browsed through some old yoga books and new spiritual books that I had brought with me from England as I needed to find some faith and reassurance. I began reading *Autobiography of a Yogi* by Paramahansa Yogananda which teaches us about the science of yoga and the Divine Babaji who is the greatest yogi to ever walk the earth. It is such an intriguing, inspiring book and it changed me enormously, giving me awareness about who I truly was. I cried when it was finished and through my tears of frustration and yearning I repeatedly *asked God for self-realisation and enlightenment!*

I then started contemplating my whole existence

and felt that I had lost myself in my relationship and in life! I didn't really know who I was, I didn't really love myself and I seemed consumed by the false, dishonest identity of my lower nature. Also, even though I had been teaching yoga for many years, I did not feel like a true yoga teacher, I felt like an imposter! For I was completely out of alignment with my soul, with my source and with God; I knew I had to develop self-examination and self-study so I could transform and be happy with me. I realised that the things I had subjected myself to when I was younger had forced me to develop a strong protective barrier around my emotions and that through my fear, unworthiness and guilt I kept many thoughts and feelings inside. I had buried the true me and forgotten about the sacred feminine within and its nurturing, compassionate, loving ways of thinking, feeling and being.

I had done everything for my partner, putting his needs before my own and living by his strong, male ego which was chaotic, selfish and overpowering, and which battled with my ego causing conflict and discontent. Yet even though my partner was controlling and never seemed to listen to me, it was my fault too as I should have expressed my emotions and told him the truth – because the truth sets us free! When we are dishonest and afraid we look for love and approval from outside of ourselves, not from the true self within, but relying on other people to make us feel good will only lead us into unhappiness. Our happiness must come from ourselves and from knowing that we are not this physical body or egoic thinking mind, but are Eternal Spiritual Souls!

I understood that I am part of the same *Divine Essence* that's within us all; however living in this physical world of duality I had created the mind-made ego personality which is the false, separate self that feeds on the negativity of my mind and the selfish pleasures of my body, forgetting about the spiritual pleasures of my soul which are infinitely greater. The ego thinks, *who I am is my job, my religion or my political group or who I am is what I own – my car or my money, and the more material things I accumulate, the more important and happier I will be*. This egocentric thinking allows children to get brought up with the beliefs of 'I need to get more things, no matter what I do to get them' and 'I have to be the best, no matter whom I hurt along the way' which leads to inequality and aggression with others. For our ego is always taking, complaining and needing; it makes us think that we are better than everyone else, that we are separate from everyone else and ultimately that we are separate from God. This duality and separation is the cause of human suffering.

Each and every one of us wants to keep the physical body healthy and to fulfil our material goals, and it is natural for us to want to do better and have prosperity, abundance and the physical things which sustain our lives. Yet fear fuels the ego to control us and our false, taking nature is never satisfied as it constantly desires more and more things to make it happy then it becomes bored with them and searches for the next thing to give it its 'material fix'! When I am attached to things, I know it's my ego moving me away from my true self within where I regret the past and become anxious about the future which leads to unfulfilled desires and problems that cause me mental stress. Once I am stressed out, I am not in harmony with this moment therefore I am not in harmony with myself and am constantly wanting to be some other place, either in the past or the future – just not here now! Medical scientists have shown that many physical problems and illnesses are caused by wrong thinking and mental stress. My ego and stress can show up in me as resentment, worry and frustration and if I keep listening to the negativity inside my head I miss out on the beauty all around me! I must see:

> "Thinking as a tool that I use, not as who I am,
> For I am not what I think,
> I am the peace, the presence, the awareness and the true self behind my thoughts"

At that time I knew I needed some down-to-earth advice so I called up my girlfriends in England and told them how I was feeling. I revealed to them that my partner had left me and they all thought it was wrong of him and viewed concerns and worries about my relationship which I sensed too. It helped immensely to have them listen, but the phone was a poor substitute to seeing them in person and giving them a heartfelt cuddle! Subsequently I moved all our possessions and my three daughters into our new house by myself. It was late February with freezing cold fog that came down, completely surrounding the house, making it very difficult to see anything and dampening all of our moods. Ripatransone is located 500 metres above sea level and has lots of snow, fog and rain in the wintertime because it's quite close to the mountains. None of us realised how cold the winter could be in this area because we had not researched the area properly! Our house had an open fireplace where we burnt old wooden furniture we found to keep warm and several radiators fuelled by diesel from an ancient boiler that somehow still worked. Yet even though it was cold, some days we got amazing blue skies and if you sat out of the wind, the sun was quite pleasant.

On one such day I took my three daughters to the local tourist office as we wanted to explore our little town. We discovered that Ripatransone is one of the oldest centres of the province of Ascoli Piceno in the Marche region on the Adriatic coast of Italy. It has been a rich, historic and artistic jewel of a town since 1571 that produces excellent organic wines, fruits, vegetables, olive oil and has six museums. We visited one spectacular art and sculpture museum within an old palace that played opera music as we walked around its timeworn rooms and went inside the local theatre that looked like it had emerged from the Shakespearean era. We also checked out the incredible open-air amphitheatre where opera was performed every July. As I descended down the aged ragged stones into the grand circle, I dreamed of sitting under the stars with a glass of wine on a lovely warm summer's night and being mesmerised by the Italian opera – what a cultural delight for my senses!

While my partner was away I did a lot of thinking about our chaotic relationship. Through the years my partner and I had some terrible arguments, with him winning and me being passive to try to keep the peace!

Yet if he had been more aware and seen me as more of an equal, if we had been true friends to each other without all the attacking negative thoughts and if we had both been liberated enough to reveal our true selves where there is only giving, forgiving and wanting to enhance one another, it could have been a *true connection*, not an egoic one. Still, now I was changing. I was awakening and consciously thinking and becoming aware of myself. I was calming down and learning to control my emotions, not wanting to overreact to the outcome of situations and I did not like aggressive arguments any more! I began focusing on me and realised that it's not about how others think of us; it's *how we think about ourselves*! I began listening to me and appreciating me, and I craved tranquillity, silence and solitude with no more egoic chaos!

Most of us live our lives in an impulsive, chaotic way, pleasing and gratifying our senses without stopping to consider the repercussions of our actions. Our five bodily senses are hearing, touch, sight, taste and smell. They pick up sense perceptions from our surroundings which our lower mind automatically reacts to and thus we perceive a physical limited reality. Yogic psychology tells us that our uncontrollable senses keep us attached to this temporary world of 'Maya' which in Sanskrit means material illusion, and if we do not awaken to the negative delusions of the mind and body they will get in the way of our spiritual development and lead us into unhappiness. Maya blinds us from seeing the light of truth within and prevents us from using our sixth sense which is our intuition and inner guidance from our heart and soul, where we perceive a spiritual limitless reality.

The Ancient Yogis tell us there are two aspects, two worlds within creation. The Absolute, Spiritual World of Eternal Life which is divine love and oneness, and then there is the Relative, Physical World of Individual Life which is fearful and segregated. Thus Maya is the illusion of only seeing the false physical fear aspect and not the true spiritual love aspect. All of physical life is changeable and impermanent, it's in a continuous dance of creating, evolving and dissolving, and has frenzied highs and lows, pleasures and pains and gains and losses with good and bad consequences. This is the Feminine Yin, Shakti and the Masculine Yang, Shiva which are the two opposing, but complementary energies or dualities in this universe. Therefore life is full of paradoxes and constantly shifting us between the positive and negative – it's the pull of the spiritual and the pull of the physical within us all!

This is how I felt; this chaotic struggle between my kind, giving nature and my unkind, taking nature was pulling me in different directions. I seemed confused and frustrated and when my partner's friend called to say he had persuaded my partner to come back to me and the children, I was relieved! When my partner arrived home, we kissed and made up as I still felt love between us, and because we had our gorgeous daughters and were beginning our new dream life, I decided to put my concerns about our relationship aside for now... However deep within, my heart sensed the truth and I knew it was in trouble!

A few weeks later, our furniture that had been in storage arrived from England and we all helped to unload the enormous lorry and things seemed a lot better between the whole of our family. My parents had rented a little apartment in a complex by the beach while they waited for their house to be built. They were the only English people living there and one night someone managed to climb up four floors, and walk through the unlocked balcony doors into their apartment. They found my dad's keys which were inside the pocket of his trousers and stole his new car with all his tools, binoculars and fishing equipment which were still in the boot. The police eventually found their car in Naples and my parents then had to take a five-hour bus ride to retrieve it. Not a good first taste of Italia!

My partner and I then decided to buy an Italian computer and I had fun accessing information from all over the world and searching the internet for spiritual guidance. The more I explored the more it confirmed everything I already felt! How humanity is destroying our magnificent Mother Earth, how we disrespect each other, how we abuse our fellow animal beings, and how our misguided materialistic society and selfish behaviour has caused a lack of spiritual values and a lack of community which has led to the decline of loving families and caused our children to be brought up as takers, not givers!

God has given us free will, has given us choice, yet with our own fearful thoughts, egotistical actions and uncontrolled minds we have created our negative selves, destructive relationships and the unpleasant things in this world all by ourselves! For we are plundering our natural resources, polluting our environment, harming our ecosystems and damaging our atmosphere which causes imbalance to the natural cycles, rhythms and energy vibrations of our planet and affects the weather causing more natural disasters. We are cutting down our sacred rainforests that hold the cure to every disease to make room for animal agriculture and palm oil crops so people can eat more steaks and snacks, and in the West we have far too much excess and stimulation as most of our illnesses are due to over-consumption, excessive indulgence and extreme stress.

Our world is greatly strained by war, starvation and poverty. For it is run on money and profit with big wealthy corporations and banks exploiting the poor and hoarding money, food and resources. This causes economic inequality and debt, and brings suffering and despair to the masses which leads to more crime, more violence and more scarcity. Furthermore, throughout human history the stronger nations have always dominated and taken advantage of the weaker ones, and because of so-called 'progress and modernisation' we have wiped out most of our indigenous cultures and lost many species of plant and animal life which has brought disharmony to nature, and thus threatens our own survival because every human being is a part of this *Natural World*!

I saw that even though humanity is advancing technologically, our old beliefs, outdated values, misplaced morals, and redundant systems and ways of living are not working for us or *'Evolving us Spiritually'*. We have collectively created everything we see with our wrong thinking as our vision of the truth has been hidden by the material cravings of the ego and its chaotic ruling –

not by the loving laws of the Universe, God. Our world is out of balance because society has been overpowered by the masculine, fearful nature with its strong ego and aggressive ways of being... yet I could see that this was forcing us towards positive change, as now we must bring the world back into balance and live more by the feminine, nurturing nature with its gentle, loving ways of being because feminine energy is vital for the spiritual evolution of us all. Thus to bring back equality which means equal opportunity for everyone, we need the kind, sharing values of all the mothers and the protective, providing values of all the fathers in our society to be in harmony!

Then just before the builders started work on both our houses... I found out I was *pregnant* with my fourth child! It was bad timing because we were about to renovate and build our yoga retreat, but I was determined to have my baby as I knew this was the boy that I had secretly wished for! I didn't tell anyone except my partner who was overjoyed that he was so fertile and when I told him I thought it was a boy, he was ecstatic! As an Italian man he had wanted a boy from the very first time I had been pregnant. In England, when we found out the first two babies were girls he was disappointed and then the third time it was a girl he became so upset he walked out of the scanning room leaving me on my own with the shocked doctor! Therefore this time we decided to pay for a private scan here in Italy that could tell the sex of the baby at three months. At the appointment my partner passed back and forth across the waiting room floor, asking me every five minutes,

"Are you sure it's a boy?" The pressure was on and I was very nervous!

The clear picture of our healthy baby came up on the scanning screen and the female doctor told us, although the baby was still so young and she could not be 100% sure, she thought it was a boy! My partner couldn't believe it, tears welled in his eyes and he jumped up hugging the Italian doctor and shouting at all the nurses that he was going to have a son... I wondered and hoped whether this baby could help solve some of the problems between us. When we arrived home we told our three daughters that they were going to have a brother and they were really excited. I could tell my dad was secretly pleased to have a grandson, yet my mum, who had guessed because of my extended belly, was ever the practical, negative one, saying what a bad time it was to have a baby and how would we cope building the houses with four children to look after! I didn't care about all the negativity or what anyone said, I was joyful and felt my family would be complete.

Why is there so much negativity in our world today and why are there so many unhappy, lonely people? It's because man and woman have forgotten who they truly are! All of us have forgotten that we are 'Divine Loving Beings'; we have lost our oneness with each other and the natural world and we have forgotten our connection with Spirit. Our responsibility must be to remember our love within and to renew our oneness and connection again because by individually contributing to the world in loving ways this helps the advancement of us all. We can learn a lot from our ancient ancestors and from some of the indigenous peoples who have lived peacefully on earth a lot longer than our modern civilisation, as they have a profound *oneness* with all things! They have *love awareness* and care for each other, feeding and giving protection to the whole of their tribe. They look after and conserve their environment, keeping the forests green and lush and they give back to Mother Earth. For they know:

> "What is done for one is done for all and
> Oneness is a compassionate state of mind
> that heals everyone!"

The more thoughts and feelings of love awareness and oneness I had, the more I would stay with my true positive self, and the more thoughts and feelings of ego unconsciousness and separateness I had, the more I would stay with my false negative self. I could see that if I allowed negativity to take me over I would end up living in more negative chaos as the law of karma states that 'every action I make travels out into the world creating more of the same and comes back to affect me'. I then had an astounding realisation! Living in chaos was awakening me and helping me to choose a more harmonious, peaceful life which is the same for us all because:

> "The chaos and suffering which is in our world today is
> Bringing us to the brink and forcing us to change!
> Out of chaos order will come; this is the
> Yin / Yang of life!"

For we can have it *ALL!* Each and every one of us can live out our spiritual and material goals, if we can just have a little self-discipline over our incessant craving for more power, more profit and more prominence which we think will make us feel safe, secure and happy. We then have time to seek *spiritual fulfilment* and to have oneness with others which brings us true safety, security and happiness! If we can try to let go of our selfish attachments and change them into the selfless attachments of being kind and helping others benefit from our spiritual and material goals, this is the path to light and wisdom because what we give to others we also give to ourselves!

I knew then that my search for meaning had to go within – for nothing in the outside world could ever satisfy my spiritual longing! Having understood this, I felt I was slowly letting go of my attachments and I was slowly learning to accept myself. I even sensed an acceptance in my relationship, thinking that for the sake of our children we could try and make it work.

I began to have a renewed faith in myself and in humanity as, under all the materialism, I felt an emerging kindness within people. Under all the fear, I felt the yearning for a peaceful society and under the separate ego I felt the oneness that we all truly want. I realised that if we join together with the power of the people, we can correct the mistakes of our past, end our suffering and recreate the future of Mother Earth for our children. All we need to do is listen to our truth within and to other people's sacred points of view; to use our free will, thoughts, feelings and choices positively and responsibly and most importantly to have a change of mind and a change of heart. For only when we remove the fear, unkindness and distrust within ourselves can we help all people, all species and our beloved planet. Only then will we see that we are:

"One Planetary Family which joins together in peace, love and unity for the good of all.
For we are Amazing Beings, we just have to realise it!"

CHAPTER 3

THE DREAM GOES WRONG

We are all part of the same Divine Essence, but thinking only of our personal desires and of the few people around us, we then experience ourselves as something separate from this essence which makes us feel bad. Cultivating compassion for all living beings gives us unity and makes everyone feel good. So let's set ourselves free to love all unconditionally and let's see the kindness within each other. Let's look for the emotions that make us all feel better and let's do the things that give us faith in the Sacred Connection of every Life on Earth!

JOANNE LEE PHILPOT

Living in this rural region of Italy I was surrounded by nature's peaceful presence and its rhythms, cycles and vibrations, and I could sense the pranic life-force energy from the forests and hillsides energising me. Springtime is wonderfully warm and glorious with all the pretty wild flowers growing in the fields and their sweet-smelling fragrances wafting through the air. The beautiful blossom hangs abundantly on the trees ready to be magically turned into delicious fruit and the first buds of grapes in the vineyards and olives on the trees begin to show. The area is amazingly green and lush due to the large amount of rainfall throughout the year and I loved to see the tropical bamboo plants growing high by the side of the roads. I had never lived in such plentiful countryside and I felt its intrinsic loveliness to be exceptionally tranquil and serene.

In town I found the local Ripanian people to be delightful! They were extremely friendly and always the first to say 'Buongiorno', which means 'good day', but there the conversation stopped as, unfortunately, my Italian was limited. There was only a small community of foreign people that lived here and hardly anyone could speak English. Many of the locals liked the quiet life and didn't seem to want change or progress. Lots of the younger people had moved to the bigger cities and left the older generations to tend to the farms or stay at home behind their closed shutters giving me the impression they were living fifty years behind the rest of Italy. Almost all the people in Ripatransone are Catholics with religious festivals going on throughout the year. They would sing and dance to the traditional Italian music which went on late into the night and, of course, taste the delicious homemade foods and drink lots of local wine.

The Ripanians have such remarkable scenery; for it is visually one of the most extraordinary places I have ever had the pleasure to live in. The view of the mountains is such an incredible sight as it seems to change and become even more astoundingly spectacular as the sun moves position throughout the day. The people here have all grown up together and gone to school together, so being an outsider I found it difficult to fit in sometimes. However I didn't mind as I preferred staying at home enjoying the peace and practising yoga, meditation and studying my books. When my retreat was finished I hoped to have enlightening talks with yoga guests from all around the world.

While reading my yoga books again after so many years I felt their ancient wisdom awakening me! The oldest literature on yoga is the Vedas and Upanishads and the Bhagavad-Gita which dates back 5,000 years, and is one of the most influential books I have ever read and a magnificent manual for humanity. Once more I became captivated by the insights of the enlightened ones that tell us everything in our world and universe is manifested and connected by prana. This *Cosmic Love/Light Energy* is in the sunlight that keeps us warm and illuminates our world, it's in the sun-ripened food we eat, in the water we drink and in the air we breathe. It's in the space between worlds which bonds our cosmos together and it animates all beings with consciousness and life as prana is the divine intelligence within all things.

Our entire universe is a single living organism and the whole of creation is constantly changing, flowing and corresponding with universal cycles which affect the cycles of our earth and the cycles within us. The sun influences seasonal changes and the moon influences the flow of the seas' tides which affects our moods and emotions. Everything interrelates with everything else in the natural world; trees and plants absorb *pranic sunlight energy* then animals and people feed upon them. All beings and ecosystems need each other to maintain life on earth and all things exist in perfect patterns of harmony together and are ultimately controlled by prana which forms the five basic elements of Earth, Fire, Water, Air and Ether (Space) from which this material universe has evolved.

The Ancient Yogis tell us there is an *eternal cycle of life* happening in every moment and nothing is lost or ever really dies! All things change, evolve and transform into new things. New planets are born from the dust of exploded stars and the atoms that make up the stars, sun, rocks, trees, lakes, animals and human beings are made of the same pranic life-force energy of our creator. When physical life comes to an end the soul consciousness transcends into the spiritual realm and the material body decays over time. Its atoms of matter then go back into the earth from where they came millions of years ago to change, transform and recycle back into the energy of earth, fire, water, air and ether, which manifests different forms of life over and over again.

> "Therefore *existence is everlasting,* all things are divinely connected and we are made of stardust and part of the whole universe!"

Our first job reconstructing the house was to hire a local man with heavy equipment to knock out the cement wine vats on the ground floor of the main house as it had been used as a cantina (winery) and for keeping animals and tractors in. It opened up a massive area to put in a new kitchen diner, huge living room and big utility with downstairs bathroom. Towards the end of the day when the man had finished, we were clearing the dust and rocks away and I felt my neck where I have worn my OM symbol necklace for fifteen years, but it wasn't there!... OM is the sacred sound of God and Creation! It is the vibration of the universe and according to the yogic scriptures, the absolute positive truth. NASA has now recorded the sound of the sun and its sound is OM. Amen is derived from OM and in yogic practice we chant it at the beginning and end of class which purifies the body, making one feel spiritually inspired. I was upset about my necklace as I thought it was lost forever and it seemed to be a sign for me, saying, "Watch out, life may not go the way you want it to!" We searched everywhere and I went to bed thinking I would never see it again. The next morning, as I was walking up the driveway, I saw something shiny in the dirt and there it was! It had been driven over a few times by the cars but I gave it a wash and it was fine.

In June, my partner's stepfather came up from Naples with two Moroccan and two Italian builders to start work on the houses; they were all friendly men who stayed in the front part of our house during the week and went home on weekends. They loved playing with the children and we helped them out with the smaller jobs on the house and tried out our Italian on them. My mum and I had to cook lunch and dinner for thirteen people every day in the smallest, hottest kitchen. In Italy, lunch is not a quick panino sandwich; lunch is a three-course affair with wine, pasta, meat or fish, and dessert or fruit. I was six months pregnant and we had fans blowing out hot air over us and sweat running down our faces! In the middle of July it became even hotter and with the children off school for their summer holidays, to keep cool we'd drive through the countryside past thousands of bright yellow sunflowers to the sandy beaches and make sandcastles, sunbathe and swim in the emerald-aqua sea that sometimes became the temperature of a luxuriously warm bath.

In August there was an African wind that came up from the south. One night, being pregnant, I felt uncomfortable in my sweltering bedroom so I went outside to try and cool off, but instead had hot wind blown in my face! The next day, while sunbathing in the garden and tanning my big belly, a black snake, about three and a half feet long, slithered past nearly touching my toes; I jumped up so quickly I nearly broke my waters! On cooler days we'd walk to our favourite field near the house to have a picnic lunch in the shade of a tree and gaze at the picturesque view of the abundant green valley with old brick farm houses and shimmering sunlit sea. We all said we could live here forever, as it was so peaceful and the perfect place for our yoga retreat!

At that time we had a lovely visit from the local Catholic priest who got out of his tiny Fiat car in all his priestly robes. He had come to bless and protect us from all the building work that was going on and proceeded to douse the house and children's foreheads with holy water. He gave us a little Italian prayer, welcoming us to the community, and I think hoping we would join his congregation… None of my family is religious. I was not christened and the closest I ever came to the church was going to a wedding or to someone's funeral; God or spiritual disciplines were never spoken of and just completely ignored. In my family I am the only person who has strong spiritual beliefs and sometimes I do find it difficult to deal with other people's views and their negativity. I understand it's just fear, doubt and the ego that is stopping them from seeing the truth, and I am always trying my best not to be judgemental as we are all at different levels of realisation and we are all awakening, some quicker than others!

Why do we believe in our mistaken society that judging, criticising and cheating others is normal, and that feeling depressed, guilty and lonely is natural? This is not normal or natural; it's merely wrong belief and incorrect thinking. I would often be very judgemental about my colourful past and put myself down, yet constant judgement of ourselves makes us think we are unworthy and not good enough to have happiness in our lives. I knew I had to be in the present moment a lot more because, when I am present, judgement cannot exist, as judgement always comes from my past experiences and conditioning. I wished people could be here now and stop judging themselves and each other. I wished we could allow others to make their own choices, decisions and mistakes because none of us are perfect. I wished we could stop relying on what others have said or on some of society's outdated beliefs and misplaced morals, and I wished we could virtuously think for ourselves, relying on the wisdom of our own inner guidance and feel faith, trust and worthiness which are our true natural emotions.

Learning to be virtuous in every thought and feeling takes constant observation, repetition and practice until our minds are familiar with virtue and it becomes spontaneous to act in a virtuous, loving way all the time. Each and every one of us has the potential true self within to be calm, worry-free and stress-free people, and to be kind, giving self-realised beings who want to help others awaken and bring love into the world. This is the *divine purpose* of each individual soul and, once we accomplish this, other people will then accomplish it because what we give to ourselves we also give to others!

We had lots of work to do on the houses and on our land which was so overgrown it took us weeks to cut the overgrown weeds down. My dad and partner built an outside decking area that we surrounded with palm trees and tropical plants. The children enjoyed playing on it and our guests would use it to perform yoga in the sunshine with the majestic view igniting the passion in their hearts. The building work carried on with everything in a constant mess and covered in dust! I was heavily pregnant by now and some mornings I'd be woken up by friendly singing coming from the Moroccan builders as they walked past my bedroom door with wheelbarrows full of slushy cement that dripped everywhere to lay the new floors. To have a shower in the tiny bathroom there was a hole in the floor for the water to drain and a flimsy shower head which was disastrous. Later on we would renovate it; however I wanted a bath to ease my back and big belly. So I came up with a great idea. I borrowed from the builders a clean, three-foot-wide yellow plastic cement bucket that I filled up with hot water from the shower. Immersing myself and just barely fitting inside, it was heaven! I also used it to bathe the children and emptied it with a saucepan.

My fourth pregnancy had been a lot tougher than my other ones. I felt sick most of the time and the last few months my back ached, but I still managed to do some yoga asanas and meditation which gave me relief and helped me to sleep. As I couldn't help build the house any more, to fill my time I would read. My dad had made me a metal and wood bookshelf that attached to the wall in the living room which looked exceptionally grand. I bought precious English books off the internet for my ever-increasing library and I couldn't wait to receive them in the post. I ordered a couple of books by the Dalai Lama which made me contemplate the controversial subject of religion.

The Dalai Lama tells us:

"My religion is very simple, my religion is kindness"

All countries, cultures and religions are different which is what makes our amazing planet so diverse. Yet throughout human history many governments have been the cause of oppression and suffering, while many religions have been the cause of fear, segregation, most of our wars and the repression of women because governments and religions are man ego-fear-made, not God love-made. Most religions are outdated as they are based on teachings that were given over 2,000 years ago and which are not relevant to us today. These teachings have been altered through the years and lost their original message and true meaning – thus they hinder our conscious evolution. Humanity must learn to have *unity in diversity!* For there is only *one creator, one God* which is being expressed throughout the world in many different ways and there are numerous paths to reach enlightenment which is the truth of God within – each path may be different but they are all equally sacred! I believe every religion has to evolve just like the rest of the world or pass away and they must all spiritually empower each individual to express the love inside and to unite people and put an end to conflict!

Whatever religion, non-religion or spirituality we believe in, every single one should assist us in following our hearts, following our truth and giving us faith in ourselves as Divine Loving Beings, because by thinking, feeling, speaking and acting upon this truth we *'Become this Truth Now!'* The truth of every faith and creed must be to raise human consciousness; to transform our minds so we are honest and accepting and forgiving and compassionate towards all beings, and to make this world a more peaceful, love-filled place. This is the meaning of spirituality and, I believe, as humanity's awareness heightens, *practising spirituality* will take over organised religion.

Anthony Douglas Williams tells us in his book *Inside the Divine Pattern*:

> *"Spirituality does not come from religion.*
> *It comes from our Soul!"*

Yoga is not a religion, yoga is the union of all religions, all faiths, all nationalities and all people and the natural world. It helps us *accept* and *respect* every spiritual discipline and it teaches us how to live our lives in a moral, ethical, yogic way so as no harm may come to us or to any other being, leading to compassion for all. Years ago in many religions, meditation or having a sense of sacredness with our self and connection with Spirit was practised by the people, but has since been forgotten. These days, many of us are now being awakened by meditation as meditation cleanses the mind from limiting thoughts and opinions of ourselves and others that we have accumulated over the years, and becoming one with the love, light and peace within is the most exquisite empowering feeling of all!

At long last the due date arrived for me to have my baby and I was more than ready for our new arrival. The next evening I felt very uncomfortable and, as time went on, I knew I was in labour. I called up my partner and eagerly said, "The baby's coming, come home now!" I wanted to have my baby at home, but that's not too popular here in Italy so we rushed to the hospital with everyone reassuring me I would have an easy birth as it was my fourth child; to our joy we already knew it was a boy and were so excited to finally be meeting him. My unbelievably beautiful baby, Rocco James, was born and the wonder of holding him in my arms dimmed the fourteen hours of excruciating pain without drugs that I went through. All my yogic breathing and squatting positions which had worked so brilliantly with two of my other births (the first one had been a caesarean) seemed in vain, and at one point the doctor was getting worried as the baby appeared to be stuck and taking too long!

My partner, being a cool modern man, was brilliant throughout the whole ordeal; he was my rock as I held on to him for dear life! Yet in the end everything was OK – we were exhausted, drenched in sweat, but ecstatically happy. I believe it's so important for the man to be present at the birth of a baby, because it is truly life-changing for everyone and extremely bonding for man, woman and child. I began breastfeeding my son as I had done with all my other babies as it's so beneficial for them, and which I found to be such a fulfilling experience that also removed excess pregnancy fat from my body! When we brought baby Rocco home, all the children's grandparents – English and Italian – were there to see their first grandson and shower him with gifts!

A few weeks after the birth, my partner, who is a cocktail bar manager, began working later nights and I was becoming a single parent of four young children. Although he finished at midnight, sometimes he would go out with his friends after work or stay behind late into the night making drinks for them all. His partying and drinking seemed to be getting worse and he became depressed. He would sleep late in the mornings and if I didn't wake him up he could have slept all day long! I do not want to go out drinking or partying any more, I had enough of that when I was younger and I always had a real battle in controlling my wild ways. I am into the spiritual side of life now, for there is no better natural high than meditation and feeling its peaceful, present awareness. Anyway, how can we hear the inspirations of our soul talking to us through our inner voice when it is constantly covered up by drinking too much, taking damaging drugs, or cannot be heard over the incessant chatter of the unconscious ego? How can we feel the emotions of our higher heart when we are consumed by chaotic life dramas and negative obsessions that block and repress our emotions? I could feel a great distance growing between me and my partner, and I called up all my girlfriends in England for some much needed advice again. Every one of them said he was not the right man for me and they all thought I should not be with him any more which I was beginning to believe.

I loved my children more than anything else in the world and taking care of them on my own seemed very natural for me, except at times doing everything alone could be really stressful! Yoga is the only practice that de-stresses me and gives me a wonderful feeling of wellbeing and peace. For yoga is my love and passion and it is a magnificent, harmonious experience that has completely transformed and enhanced the way I live my life. All types of exercise are derived from yoga and on my teacher training course I was taught Hatha yoga which is the yoga of body and breath where we unite the Feminine Yin, Shakti and the Masculine Yang, Shiva aspects of ourselves. I knew that to feel good, get my body back in shape after pregnancy and have the patience to look after my four children properly I needed to do yoga as much as possible.

Once I dropped my daughters off at school and nursery and my baby boy was having his morning nap, I'd light my incense, chant OM and begin my yoga practice with relaxation. I'd lie down on my mat with eyes closed then put my attention on my toes, relaxing my toes and then on my feet, relaxing my feet. Moving up my legs, pelvis, chest and back I'd do this with each part of my body including my neck, face, head and forehead last until my whole body felt relaxed. Next I'd perform my asanas which exercise the muscles, stimulate the internal organs and endocrine glands (hormones) and open up my chakras (centres of consciousness). They bend, stretch and balance my body in certain ways to promote fitness, health, youthfulness and strength. My students in England were amazed at how fit and muscular my body was after having children, but it's all thanks to yoga and my yogic diet. The aim of asana is to cultivate a feeling of presence, suppleness and meditation.

After asanas I perform pranayama which means life-force energy control through various breathing techniques. It promotes free flow of energy throughout the system and releases blocked negative emotions. Pranayama eliminates toxins, reduces stress, delays ageing and gives deeper states of consciousness. Most people breathe incorrectly; they breathe fast and shallow with the upper lungs only which contributes to a shorter life. Breathing yogically, slowly and deeply with all the lungs brings prana into every cell of the body giving a longer, healthier life. Next I do the bandas which lock energy inside, massage the internal organs and stimulate the nerves. They make the abdominal organs more efficient, relieving constipation and indigestion and are fantastic for the reproductive organs, giving us powerful orgasms!

After bandas I practise meditation! I sit on my mat with spine straight so pranic love/light energy comes in through my head then breathe yogically which brings me into the present moment, relaxes me and slows the breath down – thus slowing the mind down. As I put attention on my breath, my consciousness withdraws from my five senses, allowing me to let go of outside disturbances and to go within. If thoughts or memories arise I try not to become attached to them, but allow them to pass away and if my mind wanders I bring it back to the breath and feel a deeper sense of relaxation. After a while I transcend the subtlest thought and memory to be in that still mind state where I come into alignment with my true self and inner being, where I feel bliss, peace and love and where I am *in communion, in prayer with God*!

When we meditate we are transforming our mind to *be truly awake, present or mindful* in everything we do; to breathe with awareness, to talk with awareness, to walk with awareness, to do the ironing with awareness and to have sex with awareness! Meditation unlocks the door of our sixth sense and enables us to use our full unlimited potential and it empowers us to seek our own infinite truth. The Buddhists tell us it's like recharging our battery where we renew ourselves with the Divine Essence and eventually one can raise the sacred Kundalini energy which is intensified prana up the spine to enlightenment. Meditation is the space between our thoughts and this thoughtless awareness is called *Samadhi* which in Sanskrit means *'Divine and Human becoming one'*.

Lastly I chant OM and relax again by breathing in positive light energy and breathing out negative dark energy from the whole of my being. My Sat Guru says if only asanas are taught in a class this is not yoga, it's just exercise which many yoga centres around the world advocate. Yoga is holistic, unifying mind, body and soul and must include asanas, pranayama, bandas and meditation. I could feel that practising yoga while pregnant had helped me stay supple and the yoga I was doing now was making my body stronger and more powerful; I felt positive and things seemed to be going well for us!

However, a month before Christmas things suddenly went drastically wrong! My partner's step-papa, our builder, came up to us pushing pieces of paper into our hands and claiming new quotes of up to three times more money on each house to complete them both. Oh no… we could not believe it! What a stupid man; he had added up the costing incorrectly, spent money on the wrong things and gone completely over our budget. There was no money left over in our bank account, as we had bought the property on his say-so from the original quotes he had given us, but because he was 'family' we never got anything in writing at the beginning. I was so upset I cried and had the awful job of telling my parents.

All work was stopped on both houses as the last of our money ran out. We gave the builders tips and said sad goodbyes, never to see them again. The architect, whom we had paid nearly €10,000 to, and who never came to the house or did any work, finally came to check over the property and said he had never seen such bad workmanship and would never work with the builder again. We then found ourselves in an awful situation as my house needed lots more work for it to be completed and the second house was half-built. My dad phoned me with distress in his voice saying, "It's all gone! All our money is gone." Everything my parents had worked so hard for over the years, moving many times, buying and renovating old houses in England then reselling them – all their money they had saved was now tied up in this property. It was so bad to hear my dad like this; my parents had come to Italy to *live the dream and the dream was now going terribly wrong.* They had to move out of their beach apartment and into the yoga guest apartment upstairs in my house with its own bathroom and mini-kitchen which my mum sweetly named 'The Little Hovel!'

What we needed was a mortgage so we could finish both houses, but mortgages in Italy were not easy to obtain because people did not buy their homes here, they either inherited them or rented apartments, and we were also in one of the world's worst economic recessions for fifty years! We needed a mortgage or a miracle!

To add to all our problems, my brother, who is a harmless soul and likes a drink sometimes, fell down a cliff walking home from Ripatransone. He rolled down about 100ft in the dark, losing his glasses and mp3 player, but luckily he still had his phone in his pocket. He called us up yet had no idea where he was so we called the police and the whole town came out looking for the English boy who fell down the cliff. They found him and the police brought him back home, still a little tipsy but without a scratch on him. He was in the local newspaper the next day, great for us!

All I kept focusing on was our half-built house

and our lack of finances! I felt totally discouraged and had fearful negative thoughts constantly in my mind. I blamed my partner's step-papa for getting us into this mess and I wondered if we could even get a mortgage. All I could do was bury myself in some books that I hadn't read and try to find some guidance! It's amazing how knowledge always comes to me when I need it the most and I believe my Angels and Spirit Guides were helping me to receive the guidance that I needed. I started reading some metaphysical and quantum healing books and more Buddhist scriptures which permitted me to see just how empowered us human/spiritual beings are – for we influence the world around us!

Buddha said in *The Dhammapada:*

"What we are today comes from our thoughts of yesterday
And our present thoughts build our life of tomorrow;
Our life is the creation of our mind"

Quantum physicists have confirmed that when we observe and put our attention on atoms it affects their behaviour – therefore each and every one of us can manipulate matter. For we are made in the image of God the Creator! Thus we are the Divine Creators of our own life experience and everything we choose, intend and focus upon will be attracted to us and manifested into our lives. I mistakenly used to think that outside influences, circumstances and other people were responsible for how I felt and for what happened to me. Yet it is me who holds the key and power over all my experiences and situations! I am consciously or unconsciously, through my positive or negative thoughts and feelings, affecting the atoms in my body and creating my pleasant or unpleasant surroundings. Thoughts and feelings give off strong energy vibrations. Good or bad, my creative mind knows no difference; everything I think and feel will end up as a situation, relationship or experience I need to go through to discover more about who I truly am.

I realised if I could allow myself to think correctly and to feel good, this means my mind, body and soul will be in alignment, and if I try to stay in that present place for most of the time then only good things will flow into my life experience as like attracts like which is the natural law of attraction. I saw that in every moment I have the choice to be at peace where I attract positive energy to myself or to be in resistance where I attract negative energy to myself and that to change the things that were happening to me, I had to change the energy vibrations I was giving out!

A week before Christmas Day, the children's nonno (grandad) came to stay with us for a few days. He had moved to Rome and had to drive over the mountains and back again before the snow made it too dangerous. I helped him cook an incredible three-course Italian dinner for my parents and the whole of our family, and it was great to have everyone together and to talk and laugh! Ripatransone looked delightful with all the Christmas lights and decorations bringing cheer to the old, medieval streets, and each year they built a magical life-size presepe – the nativity scene of baby Jesus in the main Piazza. On Christmas Eve I took the children to see the presepe and we visited the local bar so they could warm up with a delicious hot chocolate. As we walked through the door we were greeted with 'Buon Natale' which means 'Merry Christmas' and the lovely locals gave us a traditional Italian Christmas cake called a panettone and bought me a glass of Prosecco which was so kind of them!

Yet over the holidays I missed my grandmother and all my girlfriends and friends. In England I would always invite everyone to my house, make delicious food and of course dance the night away as for me Christmas was a time of celebration and having fun! However, because we had only lived in our little Italian town for a while I didn't really know anyone to invite to our house and I wasn't sure that the Italian people were up for dancing and letting themselves go!

After Christmas, the cold bleak days of winter seemed to enhance our problems even more and I felt stressed about money and worried about my parents. When I worry I am focusing on the negative and attracting that to me and when I stress I forget to have moments in my day where I meditate; where I stop what I am doing, breathe into the present moment and feel my peace within which disperses worry and stress. In my younger years I loved performing the yoga asanas, but felt a little apprehensive about being silent and going within. Now I see that I must meditate every day so I can *be* in that present state with *my true higher self* a lot more. So I can *be* first then act; so I can be joyful and peaceful first then all the consequences and results of my actions will be joyful and peaceful!

I began to see that because of my wrong thinking, incorrect perception and mistaken lifestyle, I had created myself in the opposite of what I wanted to be. Yet this was not a bad thing, as it was causing me to raise my awareness and to give out positive vibrations so I could become the compassionate yoga teacher that I did want to be. I saw that to make my dreams come true I had to *feel with my heart and listen to my soul* as this is a sacred form of prayer that will always be answered. I had to think the highest thoughts and feel the most sublime feelings about myself and others because whenever I choose something positive, whenever I choose to feel good, I am giving out love which affects the whole world and attracts back to me a *Divine Life!*

> "God knows what is in our hearts and has already given it to us.
> All we have to do is give thanks, give love first which makes space for us to receive abundance.
> This is a *secret to life!*"

CHAPTER 4

HARVESTING AND MEETING MY GURU

There never has been or will be a time when man's own nature shall cease to demand his best and foremost attention. The science of Yoga commends itself to the foremost minds of east and west. So vital is this inner science for the evolution of Human Consciousness that besides it the greatest of Human achievements pale into insignificance.

SAT GURU YOGIRAJ SIDDHANATH

My two eldest daughters had been at school in Ripatransone for quite a while and were speaking Italian and my youngest daughter had moved up to pre-school. Every morning the bright yellow school bus picked them up outside our house at 8am and dropped them off at lunchtime and they even had to go to school on Saturday mornings! The teachers were so sweet and kind; they really cared about the children and hugged and kissed them all. My girls were making lots of friends and were invited to many birthday parties. I became quite friendly with a couple of the mums, yet trying to make myself understood in Italian was difficult; before we left England to live in Italy, I had taken an Italian course and learnt some basic conversation, but to say anything deeper was beyond me.

At that time I decided I wanted to teach yoga again and try to make a little extra money. I printed some leaflets, putting them all over town and found four ladies who wanted to come to my first class with the Mayor of Ripatransone giving me a room in town to use for free. I taught the yoga classes in Italian which was quite a challenge when trying to explain meditation and breathing techniques. Luckily yoga is quite visual and by conversing with my students my knowledge of the language began to improve. The ladies were all beginners and knew nothing about the vast subject of yoga, but as they began to feel the benefits, they really enjoyed it.

In town I met a lovely English woman who had lived in Ripatransone for five years and had been practising yoga in England for fifteen years. She frequented class regularly and we became friends, having inspiring talks and philosophising on Italy and life. I taught yoga to a local artist privately in his studio and we also talked about Italian culture after class. I found the Italian people in this area to be exceedingly friendly, jovial and helpful; however some seemed overly engrossed in their appearance and worried about how others think of them. Most of their clothes were designer labels, they liked to have the best cars and I didn't understand how they could afford it all! Also while I have respect for all religions, I did feel that the Catholic religion appeared to somehow limit people here; I thought maybe they felt scared to try new things such as yoga in case *God or their next-door neighbour did not approve*! I told my Italian students that yoga is a way of life; it is a science of healthy, ethical, spiritual living that complements all religions.

Over the years, yoga and life have taught me that there is only *One Supreme Being that we are all part of, One Eternal Super Soul* which is the collective consciousness of every soul in the universe and the God and Goddess within us all. This Divine Essence is the source of all creation; it's the light that gives light to us, it's the love within every soul and it emanates pranic love energy from the spiritual world into this physical world. God is omnipresent which means it is everywhere; it's the magic in every cell and molecule and in every thought and feeling, and it's the positive and negative and the light and dark in everything – this is why we must see the *Good or God even in the bad things*. In this physical world of duality, Spirit manifests through us and wants us to experience and create wonderful lives full of happiness so we become self-realised and fulfil our purpose which helps the whole world to evolve!

For me, God Consciousness is eternally empowering and forever forgiving; we just need to awaken to the truth and see the God, Spirit, Love that resides within you, within me, and within all things!

The Native American Indians tell us that *everything has Spirit;* everything is connected to the *one vibrationary source*! Yet throughout human history we have mostly been unconscious to our connection and compassion with all living beings. We thoughtlessly cut down our sacred rainforests, the lungs of the world that take in carbon dioxide and convert into oxygen which humans breathe because we do not see that humanity's survival depends on our interconnectedness with every species on the planet. Trees are wise beings, and they are essential for maintaining human life! The fewer trees on earth mean more carbon dioxide in the atmosphere which traps heat in and increases global warming. It also means less leaves falling to the ground to fertilize the soil and with constant non-stop food production depleting even more nutrients, we have to pump the top soil full of chemicals to make crops grow until it becomes barren like a desert. This desertification is going on all over the world!

Governments, corporations, businesses and institutions need to understand that it's not about how much money or power they produce; it's about how ethical and ecological they have been in *Maintaining Life on Earth!* When we are not motivated by selfish egotistical gain, we are then able to make decisions based on the good of all beings, not just on the good of the few! This is why we need to stop living in negative chaos, wake up from our unconscious sleep, which is causing humanity's separation and destruction, and think in a more consciously loving, unifying way. This is why I am so passionate about yoga because yoga heightens our awareness to see all life as sacred; to see our spirit within as the same combined spirit within every being and to see that we are all 'One Sacred Soul, One Sacred Heart and One Sacred Consciousness sharing the One Sacred Life!'

This is an ancient eternal truth, this is our divine

connection and our true religion and this is why I want to create a yoga retreat so I can help others who want meaning in their lives to realise these truths for themselves.

Our retreat that we were trying to create was built on a small slope, surrounded in nature's splendour by bright green fields and dense forests. I felt blessed to live in such inspiring beauty; looking out from our terrace you could see for miles around and it was lovely to watch the birds create spectacular formations as they flew around the sky and to hear them sing their sweet songs. I'd wake up in the early morning to gaze out of one bedroom window as the red sun dawned over the hills to cast its salmon-colour rays over the entire valley all the way down to the sea, and from my other window I could see through the early dawn mist across the vegetable fields and vineyards to the neighbouring hilltop castle towns which gave me the sensation of being in an old romantic movie.

At the beginning of May the children treasured walking around our land at night, catching all the otherworldly fireflies in their hands. On one enchanted evening we ran outside and could not believe our eyes as every single field around our house had been blanketed with their gentle glowing lights. It was so magical, it felt like we were in a fairy's dream, and as we sat down on the grass looking up at the clear night sky, it seemed that we could see nearly every star there was, which gave us an awareness of the blissful infinity of space and mirrored the blissful infinity of our *eternal selves!* It moved me to perceive our universe as a magical, magnificent place and that we are magical, magnificent human beings who are only just finding out how to use our natural divine energy and creative power.

I felt all the bad, evil, negative things that we have created on earth slowly being evolved out of our existence because our hearts, minds, consciousness and compassion are always expanding and evolving. Our world is not getting worse; it, us and every living being are constantly changing and becoming ever more beautiful, ever more loving and ever more spiritual as we are constantly moving towards the light, towards oneness and perfection with ourselves, with each other and with the natural world. For we come from the light of the absolute, to experience the darkness and imperfection created in this illusionary realm of the relative so we once again remember what we all forgot at birth;

> "That we already are a part of the
> Everlasting Divine Light"

On our land we have fifteen olive trees, four cherry trees, two peach trees and one apple and one fig tree. The beautiful cherry blossoms came in April, then at the end of May we got the biggest, blackest most delicious cherries and I was so thankful for such overwhelming abundance! We climbed up ladders filling our overflowing baskets with them, all the children's hands and faces were stained red from eating so many and we sat and stoned heaps to make cherry pies and delicious cherry juice. Our closest neighbours down the hill are farmers. They have a large extended family and all live together in one house with the friendly older ladies working in the fields bent over all day long in the hot Italian sun or in the freezing cold rain. When my children played out on the land the ladies would give them heaps of fruit and vegetables and in strawberry season they filled their baskets with the most succulent, mouth-watering strawberries!

Time was moving on and we had to do something about getting a mortgage, but everywhere we tried was a 'No!' I went to see the Mayor of Ripatransone who was a young, free-thinking man, open to new ideas and knew our family well as one of his young daughters was in the same class at school as one of my daughters. We had written out a plan for our yoga retreat, putting all the benefits of tourists visiting Ripatransone, spending their money and using the local restaurants, amenities and produce. He thought it was a good idea and could not understand why we had so much trouble in getting a mortgage. The Mayor told us his auntie was a director in a large bank by the beach and maybe she could help us out. Off we went to the bank and the lovely lady talked about the state of the world economy, the fact that we had tried so many other banks and that our credit was not good. She was helpful as they all were; however it was another 'No' which was terribly demoralising and upsetting for us all. I felt really depressed! I looked dreadful and my body caught a really terrible cold because my mind was full of negativity.

Over the next few months I sought ever more spiritual guidance and began watching some truly inspirational films on the internet such as *Peaceful Warrior, The Secret, Kymatica* and *Thrive*. They gave me hope and reassurance in all I had learnt, confirming all my beliefs in the laws of karma, attraction and love, and in every spiritual book I had ever read which tell us 'we are living, breathing magnets pulling everything towards us and that our thoughts really do become things'. For we are the powerful creators of our own lives and the creators of our own bodies; we create them by the wholesome or unwholesome food, drink and drug substances we put inside ourselves, by our pleasant or painful thoughts and feelings and by our calming or stressful lifestyles. As a result of the pressures and imbalances created by our fast, modern lifestyle we become stressed out. Negativity of the mind and living in fear with constant worry manifests disease in the body. We then run to the doctor taking so many pills and potions that our body's own immune system becomes repressed, and we can't heal ourselves.

Our body is an outward manifestation of our inner emotional, spiritual and mental fear, confusion and conflict. I believe when we have an illness we are not sick – we are *Toxic!* Our body and mind is toxic from all the bad toxic food, drink and medicinal drugs that we have ingested and from the negative toxic thoughts and fearful feelings we continually focus on. The law of attraction and love works inside our bodies as every thought we think emits a chemical called a neurotransmitter which matches our emotional state and travels from the brain to every cell, uniting the mind with the body. Fearful, destructive thoughts and emotions emit chemicals and toxins which bring imbalance to our bodily system and change the structure of our cells. They take us away from the present moment, blocking the flow of prana within our energy system and slowing down our chakras which leads to illness and ageing. I could see that many of society's health problems had been created by fear and stress and by a lack of love and the constant pursuit of materialistic needs which abuse our bodies and the environment.

I looked at my own close and extended family and friends and saw that many of them were either physically or mentally sick in some way. Lots were ageing prematurely and had problems in life and most were not at all prosperous or happy with whom they were. I began asking, 'Why in our spiritually unconscious society do we believe that as we become older we must age quickly, become sick, lose our memory or end up senile?' To me this is just ancestral karma and incorrect beliefs which have been passed down from generation to generation throughout human history. If we look in the mirror and think, feel and say to ourselves, "I look old, I feel sick, I'm so poor, I'm unhappy or I'm unlovable," then over time we start to believe these opinions and eventually we will become them! I realised that a healthy person is in a state of *happiness* and is therefore kind, caring and of service to others, but a fearful society that has a selfish world view which denies love will produce unhealthy people who are unhappy, and therefore not kind, caring or of service to others.

I wanted to tell everyone in my family and all my friends that a healthy loving mind gives us a healthy body, and it's the body and the mind and the soul that must be healed; we must heal the whole person holistically.

Yet if I said this to my loved ones many of them would think I was crazy. They'd say, "No! It's got nothing to do with the way I think or feel or my lack of self-love; it's that person, this situation, my job, car, house, wife or God that is making my life so challenging." This is the way we have all been conditioned to think, that life has brought terrible things upon us, when in reality, through incorrect perception, we have brought and attracted everything upon ourselves! For we do not see the power we have over our situations or the magic we possess to healthily transform our bodies or the love we can all embrace to change our world view!

Later on in the year our other neighbour, who is the owner of an organic cantina, pulled up in his tractor and asked my dad if he wanted a job grape picking in the vineyards. It sounds very romantic picking grapes in the Italian sunshine, yet it is back-breaking work as most of the vines in this area are planted in 45 degree hills, and the only way up is to hang on to the back of the tractor and be hauled up. Every morning the pickers would tuck into a hearty breakfast of wine, bread, cheese, meat, cakes and coffee that the owners' wives made which they served in the vineyards, and of course gaze at the 360° panoramic view which enthralled and motivated them. One morning the wives left the basket of food covered with a cloth under a tree while the workers finished off a row of vines, but unfortunately for them the pet dogs got there first. All that was left of their breakfast were a few cakes with the two dogs lying on the ground too full to move!

After the grape picking my dad met Domenico,

a young at heart, older Italian man who spoke perfect English; he helped out everyone in town and still worked odd jobs throughout the year. He asked my dad to work with him in the olive oil factory, for about seven weeks in November and December with the factory open twenty-four hours a day. They did shifts of twelve to fifteen hours around the clock and they worked on one shift from midnight to midday which was exhausting. However to cheer them up the local farmers arrived at the factory with their olives and brought delicious plates of pastas, meats and cooked chickens. The workers had late night pizzas washed down with homemade wine and in the mornings everyone brought in coffee and homemade cakes for them. Even the nuns in their black, flowing habits from the hilltop monastery came in with hundreds of baskets of olives and more food. My dad was the only Englishman to ever work in the factory, and as he was an engineer he fixed one of the machines which had broken down and the Italians loved him!

It was then time for us to harvest our olives which were very abundant and had no worms in them. We picked the wild olive trees in the misty rain with our hands completely numb from the cold and laid out nets under the trees to catch them as they fell. We managed to fill nine baskets and my dad took them to get pressed at the olive oil factory for free, crushing them through two enormous stones and then pressing them to have thick, green, first press oil come trickling out. It made forty litres of pure organic olive oil that tasted fantastic and lasted us for nearly a year. We used it for cooking, drizzling over salads and I even used it on my wrinkles every night and on my hair to soften it; there is something exceptionally fulfilling about picking, pressing then using your own olive oil, a real treat.

As the months went by I started to see that what had happened at the bank was for the best because if we had received a mortgage at that point we would not have been able to make the repayments and subsequently we definitely would have lost the house. Everything happens for a reason and I knew this was part of my spiritual journey and my soul's path, and that I just had to have faith and keep moving forward. For I believe that yogic psychotherapy is changing my negative state of my mind so I can be open and receptive with love and positivity to receive, not closed and unreceptive with fear and negativity where I push guidance, wellbeing and abundance away!

When the negative mind is healed physical disease will dissolve. Identification with the negative egoic mind makes us feel fearful and alone as the mind becomes sick from incorrect perception, from seeing the delusions of the ego as real. Once we stop blaming outside conditions for the way we feel, take responsibility for our own state of mind and begin to heighten our vibration, we come into alignment with our true self which allows all the power of the universe and divine prana to flow through us. This changes the way we think and feel about ourselves, and gives us a younger, revitalised disease-free bodily system. For we can all go within and use the power of presence, the power of collective consciousness, and the power of God's love energy to heal because:

> "It's all in our beliefs and the way
> we perceive who we are!"

The enlightened ones tell us that if we can quieten our mind and open our heart by sitting still for a few minutes or going for a quiet walk in nature or gazing into a fire or stroking our cat or listening to uplifting music, which are all forms of being present in the moment and meditating, then we connect with this *'divine moment of pure bliss consciousness, of pure positive peace and of pure love energy'*. Where there are no fears, doubts or depressions, where there is no old age, unhappiness or illness but where bliss transforms us and our soul/love begins the healing process.

When I want to heal any pain, injury or problem in my body, first I try to identify the *fear* and wrong thinking that caused it and which is blocking me. Then closing my eyes, I breathe yogically raising my vibration and increasing my feeling of love so I connect with Spirit. The pain is a guide for me to focus all my attention upon the infected area and I consciously ask, thank and send love energy into the exact location of the pain so that *love* transforms the cells and atoms into a higher, healthier vibration. I stay with this sensation for as long as I wish, then bring prana through my feet, up my legs and hips, healing and rejuvenating every organ of my body as it travels through my chest, arms, back, shoulders and into my head, which makes me feel completely energised, purified and pain-free!

> "For feeling love is the magic emotion and being

> thankful are the magic thoughts
> that heals mind, body and soul"

At that time I began watching my beloved Sat Guru on his internet site as much as possible; he was having an enormous effect on me and giving me much needed faith and encouragement. There are many different Gurus and spiritual masters in the world and when I was living in England I was taught yoga by some fantastic teachers; yet it seemed none of them had found true enlightenment... However when I first heard Yogiraj Siddhanath speak the words;

"Earth Peace through Self-Peace"

I knew he was a *self-realised Yogi* and I felt an instant connection with him which has grown throughout the years.

We all need help and guidance and to listen to and learn from others who are wiser than ourselves, and we can all embrace change and let go of our old ways of thinking and living right now in this very moment. We can become humble from understanding the ancient, sacred teachings of others because humility helps us realise ourselves and when we do begin practising yoga, meditation or any other spiritual discipline we sense our *divinity* within. Guru is a Sanskrit word, 'Gu' means darkness and 'ru' means dispeller, so a Guru is one who dispels the darkness to bring in the light. *The Guru enlightens you and uncovers the light of your soul.* In India the tradition is to seek a Guru for training and sacred knowledge is usually handed down from Guru to student verbally. Even to this day many of the advanced techniques such as Kundalini Kriya yoga are a closely guarded secret and only passed on orally when the Guru thinks the student is ready.

The more I listened to my Sat Guru the more awakened I was becoming by his astounding wisdom and I knew I had to see him in person. Even though money was tight, I managed to get an inexpensive flight to London for a two-day workshop on Kundalini Kriya yoga with my Sat Guru. My partner and parents looked after the children and I stayed at my girlfriend's house which was fantastic! The workshop was held in a beautiful white, light-filled hall with lots of friendly, Indian married couples that had big smiles on their faces and of course lots of eager yoga enthusiasts. We were all wearing white for purity, waiting with anticipation and excited to be meeting him.

Sat Gurunath Yogiraj Siddhanath is a living Himalayan Master and a truly amazing Yogi. He is incredibly inspiring, very funny and speaks to us of the truths in life and of his unique spiritual experiences. My Guru comes from the lineage of mystical masters called the Nath Yogis. They live in the Himalayan mountains, evolving humanity into divinity and their founder is the Supreme Yogi-Christ Mahavatar Shiva Goraksha Babaji, the same Babaji introduced in the book *Autobiography of a Yogi*. Yogiraj describes in his book *Wings to Freedom* how he spent his early years in the Himalayas and was spiritually transformed by the Divine Babaji, realising the unity of all yogas and religions.

Yogiraj is a householder Yogi, he is married with children and grandchildren and his wife is also a yogini. They built the Siddhanath Forest Ashram in Pune, India which is a place for rejuvenation and have shown that in order to meditate and achieve enlightenment it is not necessary to live as a monk or a hermit, cutting oneself off from society, as we can all have a family, unite our spiritual life with our physical life and live yogically from our own homes. My Sat Guru is dedicated to the evolution of human consciousness and travels the world healing and transforming millions of people.

At the London workshop he initiated us into Kriya yoga by anointing our foreheads with perfumed oil that had been blessed and chanting OM. He taught us some of the sacred Kundalini Kriya yoga techniques and gave us the transmissions of *'Shaktipat'* which helps speed up the individual's spiritual evolution and *'Shivapat'* which is 'a stillness' when he shares his enlightened mind. Yogiraj explains Kundalini Kriya yoga, from the workshop:

"Kundalini Kriya yoga is the sacred science of the Self, and with constant practice and an open mind these higher levels of consciousness are available to each human being. Kundalini, Shakti energy is a form of Prana and lies as Light, Sound Vibrations potentially coiled three and one half times at the base of the spine. It is our Soul potential, eternal and immortal, and is awakened by scientific Kriya Yoga procedures which raise this energy up the spine, piercing each chakra. It is the swiftest and simplest way to God, enriching your life and making you experience the God within"

Kundalini Kriya yoga is a form of spinal breathing, and the upward flow of prana expands soul consciousness and the downward flow of apana dissolves negative karma. These breath currents magnetise the spine which becomes like a magnet, pulling up the Kundalini energy where it eventually transforms the mind into divine consciousness and where we realise the body as light and have union with love, with God in Samadhi. Awakening our evolutionary Kundalini energy and chakras is the birthright of every being on earth; however this powerful science must be performed under the guidance of a true Guru as it can be very dangerous.

Coming home I felt positive, energised and had been totally transformed by my Sat Guru's words and love for humanity. Every morning before the children woke up and before breakfast I practised the Kriya yoga meditations. While doing them my breath actually stops for minutes at a time, the body is sustained by all the pranic life-force energy that has been generated and my heart and bodily processes slow down, therefore during meditation I am arresting the ageing process!

A few weeks after the workshop my children became super-excited because it was time for 'Carnevale' – the carnival! Even though it was cold, everyone dressed up in funny outfits to ride on decorated floats and tractors and have fun dancing in the streets of our little town to the loud music. The adults drank mulled red wine called 'Vin Brule' that kept the cold out of your feet and the children ate traditional carnival cakes and pastries. Every school class had its own themed float and my girls dressed up as garden gnomes, chocolates and pirates with the whole town covered in crazy string and confetti which took weeks to clear up. The carnival was a lovely coming together and feeling of community for the local Ripanians; however I started to wonder if I would ever fit into their way of life, as I wanted more than local customs and religious festivals; I wanted a spiritual connection with people's hearts, minds and souls; I wanted to help them release their ego and I wanted everyone to have *oneness with each other!*

Yet I didn't think the people here in Ripatransone were evolved or spiritually free enough for this kind of change; nevertheless change is the nature of life and, even though it seemed fearful, I personally wanted to change more than anything.

Mahatma Gandhi said:

"You must be the change you wish to see in the world."

The fear of change is just the fear of the unknown and the fear of losing my identity. This fear is my ego trying to hold onto and stay attached to its false sense of 'who it is' through its outdated beliefs, old emotions and familiar possessions that do not serve it any more. My negative ego and its lower, taking nature have brought me only ignorance and frustration and have been holding me back from manifesting the life that I want. But now I am awakening to it! I am surpassing my selfish ways of behaving and I am increasing my love vibrations, and asking my Angels for guidance in overcoming my ego personality. When we become quiet and go within we hear the inner voice of truth and wisdom whispering to us from our soul. This attracts the higher light beings – our Angels and Spirit Guides that are always giving us intangible messages, ideas and inspirations for us to take action upon and make tangible in our lives. I believe our Angels and Spirit Guides are highly evolved souls from other worlds, realms and dimensions who are working for the collective consciousness to help evolve and liberate us all. Yet they cannot show themselves or help us too much because *humanity has its own evolution to work out and its own spiritual agenda*!

Eventually when I do realise my truth and discard my delusions I will transcend the limited unaware feeling of the *small fearful ME*, and replace it with an unlimited aware feeling of a *bigger loving ME*! This transition may be uncomfortable; but in order to grow and evolve I must be honest and determined to let go of this false egotistical self and allow the joyful comprehension of my true limitless self to come forth.

The more I practised my Kundalini meditations, the more I felt I was changing! For when I am in that present, still mind place of no thoughts, of not worrying about the past or future, of accepting life as it is and of *just being me,* I know this is the place of true healing, true love and my true self! This is my sacred silent place of peace where I receive divine guidance from my soul; it's where I feel alive and sense the aliveness of all things and it's my place of true happiness where I *touch divinity!*

It is very important to actually perform yoga, meditations or any other spiritual discipline regularly. One could read a million inspiring books and listen to sacred knowledge from many Gurus and teachers;

however without putting into practice or doing the inner work and self-study they suggest one may never move forward on the journey of *self-remembering*. At first it may seem quite difficult to motivate oneself, yet as with anything in life practice makes perfect. Just like when we began swimming or riding a bike, we thought we could never do it but with patience, practice and persistence we eventually mastered it.

Do not procrastinate! Seize the moment, take control of your life and with a positive attitude do what you need to do to awaken and liberate yourself. Yoga and meditation is my path, and it may be the path for you! We all have the divine potential within to be who we want to be; to be a loving, peaceful, compassionate self-realised helper of our family, helper of our community and helper of humanity, so take action now! You have the choice, it's up to you!

> "Remembering our Peace within
> is the key to bringing Peace on Earth!"

CHAPTER 5

A LUCKY ESCAPE AND OUR CHAKRAS

When life becomes challenging and things feel like they are going wrong, stop what you are doing, breathe into the now, feel your Spirit Soul within and be calm through the chaos. Consciously connect to this present moment and to the Love Energy flowing through you. Feel that Oneness of Being, feel your Inner Bliss, feel the flow of this energy revitalising your body, mind and soul, and carrying you onwards and upwards to live in Joy… giving you trust in your Eternal Self.

JOANNE LEE PHILPOT

It was an exceptionally cold winter that year. We woke up one day to find a metre of snow outside and an incredible winter wonderland as far as you could see! All the roads were thickly covered, it was impossible to drive anywhere in the car, and we were '*snowed in*'. For a week the children couldn't get to school, I couldn't teach yoga, and my partner and brother had to walk three kilometres up the steep, slippery hill to get some provisions at the local shop. It was fun to play with our dogs in the snow and to walk around the white pristine land, but I had not come to Italy to see snow; I had come for the sun! I didn't know our region could be so icy cold; I thought because we lived halfway down the boot of Italy and ten minutes' drive from the beaches, it would be warm for most of the year.

We had bought our house as a yoga retreat and needed it to be large enough for all our guests; however it was extremely expensive to heat because electricity was so expensive in Italy. We could not have two electrical heating appliances on in the house at the same time; if we had the oven and iron on it tripped the electricity switch and with two families living in one house it was always going off. I got hot water for our baths, showers and for the kitchen from a water heater in the bathroom and this also used up lots of electricity. It was cheaper to switch the water heater on at night but sometimes I would forget, having to boil up hot water to use in the kitchen and to wash the children in the morning – it felt like I was living a hundred years ago!

Next, the twenty-year-old boiler that heated the radiators in our house broke down. 'Oh No!' We had no money to buy a new one so a friend of ours, who was not a qualified plumber, tried to fix it and sometimes it worked, sometimes it didn't. We had previously knocked out and blocked up the upstairs fireplace when we were renovating the rooms for the yoga guests, which was a real shame as we could have been sitting beside a roaring fire. Consequently, we walked around the house with lots of layers on, and slept in our dressing gowns and went to sleep seeing our breath in the air. Although the winter in Ripatransone may have been shorter, I thought it was a lot harsher than in England.

When nonno came to see the children before Christmas he brought us a powerful paraffin fire that I carried around with me from room to room, trying to keep warm. My children would always complain that they were cold, poor darlings and to go to school in the mornings I had to warm their clothes by the fire with steam evaporating off them as everything was so cold and damp. We put four single beds in one room with me, my partner and the children all huddled together for heat!

We also got the terrible thick fog again which descended down over the town and countryside causing everything to be even more cold, damp and wet. It engulfed the house, trapping us all inside and making things depressingly claustrophobic. To lift my spirits I would go to my bedroom and practise Kundalini Kriya meditations and I was becoming completely fascinated with the pranic energy running through my heart, soul, chakras and energy system. I found it miraculous that the whole universe is made up of energy and every human being gives out vibrations of energy through their thoughts and feelings which travel out along the universal energy field to be expressed as words and actions that affect the whole of creation. All things are in a constant state of energetic vibration and everything is *dancing with joy from God's love energy* which connects all living beings and the entire universe as one!

We receive pranic energy each night when we sleep

and we can obtain an abundance of it while we are in meditation, but instead of looking for it inside of ourselves we take energy from each other. Humans have always felt fear and negativity which originates from the false egoic mind. This fear is the feeling of being disconnected from prana and we fight with each other over this energy, which is the cause of all human conflict. Instead of unconsciously taking energy from others, we can consciously go within and take it from the abundant source of the Universe, God.

The enlightened ones tell us that our mental health depends upon the state of our mind, upon how loving or fearful we are and upon the free flow of prana within our spiritual energy system. Thoughts and emotions are energy and it's our blocked, repressed energy which is the cause of many mental, spiritual, emotional and physical ailments. When we are young we are sometimes shown to repress our natural emotions. We are told not to cry, not to get angry, not to show fear and not to express love which causes an accumulation of painful feelings, and together with our unpleasant experiences and repressed memories they become trapped inside creating an energetic *pain-body*. This pain-body may manifest as a negative, fearful outlook on life, causing us to feel passive, depressed and helpless or aggressive, angry and selfish which every cell in our body is affected by. Performing the healing energy tools of Hatha and Kundalini Kriya yoga opens the chakras, allowing the free flow of energy throughout our system and releasing blocked negative feelings, experiences and memories from our pain-body.

One yogic form of pranic healing perfected by my Sat Guru is *Surya Yoga* which means healing with solar power from the Sun as the highest concentration of prana is found in sunlight. This incredible technique flushes toxins out of every cell and the body is permeated with life-giving prana which dissolves fear, stress and pain and retards the ageing process. It also heightens our positive magnetism which repels the negative energy of other people's thoughts and feelings. I had been performing this technique that my guru had taught me every morning out on my terrace. On blue sky winter days the magnificent sun's rays saturated my body with protective healing energy and I could feel the power of prana giving me *spiritual awareness*. I felt alive and re-energised, ready to start the day and I thought it was preposterous that the world was not using this energy wisely! For the life-force energy emanating from the sun can be harnessed and utilised with our new technology to power every country, every individual house and every electric car with free, clean, renewable energy so that every person may have a better life!

My dad is always telling me;

"Why don't the governments of the world understand the energy within our universe? Instead of using fossil fuels such as oil, gas and coal which release greenhouse gases into the air, and the carbon dioxide gets absorbed by our oceans which slowly turns them acidic and kills life; or using fracking which causes earthquakes and poisons nature or nuclear energy that is dangerous and

produces nuclear waste that man then has to dispose of underneath the ground for the next generation to deal with when it all leaks! Let's use the Sun which is our pranic energy power source or wind, water or magnetic and gravitational field energies which are clean and renewable, and let's all conserve and not deplete Mother Earth's resources any longer!"

The rich elite bankers and multinational corporations who own the fossil fuel companies and run our world have to change and stop their ceaseless selfish short-term craving for money. They must stop devouring our natural resources, stop polluting our land and seas, stop exploiting our deprived nations, stop selling us inferior food full of chemicals, stop prescribing us pills that keep us unhealthy and medical treatments that poison us, and stop making the rich richer and the poor poorer! However I could see that they would never stop, for they are an out of control machine that just consumes and takes everything Mother Earth gives! They do not want to change, as change means they will lose money or go out of business. If we allow these egoist elitists to carry on their destructive ways, like many other ancient civilisations we will destroy ourselves – Mother Earth will be renewed, but we will be gone! I could see that it is up to us individuals, the caring human beings of the world, to come together, self-governing our own communities, creating our own renewable energy and using our connection with Spirit and the positive power of prana to create a *Peaceful Protected Planet for all!*

My Guru told me that even when there was no sun I

should still do Surya Yoga as I would receive the healing benefits of prana through the clouds, and I knew this was protecting me from catching any illnesses. As some days the cold was so intense inside my house, it gave me headaches and pains all over my body and my poor mum contracted a terrible chest infection bordering on pneumonia which lasted six weeks. It got so bad I had to take her to the lung specialist and she was prescribed super-strong antibiotics. I dreamed of the good old days back in England in my lovely bungalow with the central heating on, all warm and cosy and where the electricity bills were much more affordable.

Our Italian house had been built over another older house with the walls three feet wide in areas. The new part of the house was built of cement, not bricks, and did not breathe properly, so when the house was not heated correctly the damp and condensation produced thick, black mould which stained the white ceilings and walls. Everyone in Ripatransone was an expert on the 'muffa' mould and there were lots of products to buy to try to prevent it. My parents' apartment upstairs was also cold and damp with lots of black mould in their bedroom which was not good for my mum's health. They were using an old gas cooker for heat with the oven door open, warming up the whole place quite nicely, but it soon became too expensive to use. My dad then came up with an idea to keep them warm. He made little wooden log fires in builders' cement pots and placed them in his lounge, bedroom and bathroom with the windows open and they were nice and comfortable. I went to teach my yoga class in town and when I came back I checked on my parents making sure that everything was OK.

Around 10pm I went to bed, but just as I was drifting off to sleep my dad stumbled into my bedroom, talking incoherently. I had never seen him like that before, and it seemed like he was drunk or on drugs. "Quick," he said, "I feel really funny, I feel terrible." I took his arm and raced into my parents' bedroom where I saw my mum trying to put on her dressing gown but she could not get her arm in the sleeve as she had lost all co-ordination and was mumbling. I didn't understand what was happening and shouted for my partner who is always fantastic in times of panic. He ran upstairs and when he saw them said, "Quick, to the RSA," which is the local medical centre in Ripatransone. We managed to put my mum's dressing gown on her and bundled them both into the back of the car. I stayed in the house to look after my sleeping children and had to have a glass of red wine to calm my nerves.

My partner called me from his mobile to say that they were now racing towards the hospital in two ambulances and my parents were given oxygen on the way. It was a serious situation and I was so worried I began crying and praying for them! A little later he called me again to tell me that they had been taken to the emergency room and were now linked up to lots of different machines with drips in their arms and given more oxygen therapy treatment; it was unbelievable!

My mum and dad were in the hospital for the next three days. The doctors said they had a *very lucky escape* as they had both suffered carbon monoxide poisoning from the fires. The count in their blood stream was so high that if they had gone to sleep they would not have woken up and would have died… My Goodness! I will never use the phrase 'It can't get any worse' because sometimes it does, it really does. The doctors looked after them well and the next day two policemen came to the house checking out the apartment, making sure my partner and I had not poisoned my parents! They asked questions and wanted to see where the fires had been made, and eventually they seemed satisfied and left. They must have thought we were crazy, but apparently, according to the doctors, carbon monoxide poisoning happens quite regularly here in Italy!

"Through your suffering you shall be raised up"

When life becomes challenging I do feel fortunate because I have yoga, my Guru, spiritual books and trust in love energy to help me understand why things happen. At the time everything seems hopeless, yet if I can have faith that out of every bad situation something good will come, and that I am learning something which is helping me to evolve, then things do not always seem so terrible. My spiritual books tell me that eventually I will turn negative situations into enlightening experiences, by not resisting what is going on in the moment, but by accepting things as they are happening. Whether they are good or whether they are bad I must let it all be and surrender to it so I do not become consumed by the drama or affected by the outcome! Anyway, going through the bad things is important because it makes me want, ask and thank Spirit for all the good things.

As always, to take my mind off things, I sought refuge in my books and through my fascination with prana I began studying yogic physiology again. I found it incredibly interesting that every human being has an invisible energy system made up of interrelated light energy or astral bodies which range from the subtlest – the spirit/soul body, emotional body and mental body – down to the densest physical body. I discovered that when some Buddhist Lamas and Yogis reach enlightenment just before death, their physical body diminishes, leaving a Rainbow Body of Light and Kundalini Kriya Yoga and many spiritual books tell us that, as humanity evolves, we will all ascend into our light energy bodies!

The energy bodies form the magnificent *Souls Aura* which is our electromagnetic field that's within us and surrounds us. We attract and give out energy vibrations through the magnetism of our auric field and our thoughts, feelings, dreams and visions determine whether it is positive or negative. Our aura is fed by prana from the 72,000 nadis (channels) that run throughout the energy system. The nadis radiate out from the chakras and the main nadi is called Sushumna which runs along the spinal cord. Our chakras absorb and distribute prana through the universal energy field which connect us to the earth's chakras and to the seven planets in our solar system which are enormous chakras that connect us with the whole universe; thus everything is joined by *God's Love Energy*.

Chakra in Sanskrit means wheel or vortex and there are seven main chakras located inside the spine, on Sushumna nadi. They influence our physical, psychological, emotional and spiritual wellbeing, sending us messages through our thoughts, feelings and perceptions. Each one represents an essential issue and has its own vibrational seed sound which, when chanted, purifies and opens the chakra. Prana moves through the chakras where it is distributed to the physical organs, cells and to the glands of our endocrine system which regulate the body's hormonal functions. In a healthy person the chakras are open, spinning fast and in alignment with each other which allows free flow of prana up the spine, but if they become blocked the hormones do not secrete which leads to deterioration, illness and ageing.

At each chakra there are a number of *Lotus Flower* petals formed by pranic energy vibrations. Medical science today tells us that the number of petals corresponds with the major trunk nerve endings within the physical body. The Lotus Flower was chosen for symbolic representation by the Ancient Yogis because it thrives in dirty water and was considered miraculous that a beautiful flower could grow in such conditions; evolving and raising itself up out of the water into the light. This is the same for us human beings as we *breathe and think Kundalini, Shakti* energy up Sushumna channel it penetrates each chakra, speeds up their vibration and opens the lotus petals to evolve our consciousness. As it rises upwards towards heaven it unites with *Shiva* energy and eventually reaches Sahasrara, the one thousand-lotus petal chakra above the head. When these two energies converge, it is the union of

Yin and Yang, of Feminine and Masculine and the blessed marriage of Heaven and Earth where we experience enlightenment!

As I had been meditating and raising the Kundalini energy up my spine for quite a while, I began to have amazing things happen to me! A couple of weeks after my parents came out of hospital, I was in my sacred little yoga room which is the only place I can go to have complete peace and quiet, since my house is always so noisy with my four young children playing games, listening to music and singing and dancing their hearts out. While I was in one of my yogic asanas and being in a peaceful meditative state, I looked at my body and began having *true vision* because I could see a white and blue light surrounding my hands, feet and legs... It was astonishing! I was seeing my *soul's aura* for the first time and it really excited me! Also during meditation I started to feel a tingly sensation at the top of my head so I called up my yoga friend in London to find out what this was and he said it was Ajna, my third-eye chakra opening!

I realised that through my years of yoga practice and more recently through my Kundalini Kriya meditations I was speeding up my chakras to regain youth and vitality, I was purifying my heart chakra to experience the world as *loving not fearful* and I was opening my third eye to finally see the *truth of life!* I saw that when I feel good and connected, my chakras are open and distributing and converting spiritual energy into physical energy which is how I magically transform my thoughts, feelings and intentions into my physical reality!

It does not matter which spiritual discipline or religion each person on this planet follows, they will all raise Kundalini energy up the spine through the chakras towards *'Self and God realisation'*. In Egyptian mythology many pharaohs and Gods were depicted with awakened serpent energy moving up the spine, piercing the eye of Horus or Ajna Chakra, the third eye. In the Mayan and Aztec traditions, ancient stone carvings show the winged serpent God which represents the awakened evolutionary consciousness and in Christianity Kundalini energy is the *Holy Spirit!*

I learnt a great deal about our chakras and made a list explaining their meaning.

Muladhara the Root Chakra is at the base of spine by the genitals, its colour is red and mantra Lam. It influences the prostate gland, lower spine, bladder and colon. It is the centre for physical survival, security, money and basic material needs. If this chakra is blocked one may be immersed in Maya-material delusions, be fearful, selfish, hold onto old beliefs from family or religions and react from the pain-body. Physical problems are bowel, bladder, leg or feet issues. When open, we feel safe and fearless. 4 petal lotus.

Svadhisthana the Sacral Chakra is in the spine by lower abdomen, its colour is orange and mantra Vam. It influences the reproductive glands, kidneys and menstrual cycle and corresponds to the moon. It is the centre of sexuality, creativity, attraction, relationships and emotions. If this chakra is blocked one may fear change and lack emotional support. Physical problems are sexual dysfunction, depression or addictions. When open one gives and receives sensual desires openly, and releases blocked emotions to feel positivity. 6 petal lotus.

Manipura the Navel Chakra is in the spine at the solar plexus, its colour is yellow and mantra Ram. It influences the pancreas gland, stomach and liver. It is the centre for will power, ambition, ego, self-esteem and controls metabolism and digestion. If this chakra is blocked one may feel shame, be angry, irritable, lack confidence and use people to satisfy personal needs. Physical problems are ulcers, liver and digestive issues and diabetes. When open we feel a sense of purpose and feel contentment and trust. 10 petal lotus.

Anahata the Heart Chakra is in the spine at the sternum; its colour is green and mantra Yam. It influences the thymus gland, heart and circulatory system. It is the centre of, self-love, joy, nurturing and compassion, and unites the lower chakras of matter with the upper chakras of spirit. This is the Lotus of the Heart as the heart sends out the strongest signals of love and attraction. If this chakra is blocked it stops the flow of love energy. One may feel unworthy of love or afraid of being emotionally hurt. Physical problems are heart attack, high blood pressure and asthma. When open one aligns with the heart to feel love for self and all beings. 12 petal lotus.

Vishuddha the Throat Chakra is in the spine at the hollow of the throat; its colour is blue and mantra Ham. It influences the thyroid gland, throat, mouth and voice. It is the centre of communication, self-expression, truth, faith, singing and writing. If this chakra is blocked one may not express emotions freely. Physical problems are sore throat, thyroid problems and ear infections. When open we express ourselves truthfully and become deep listeners. We trust in the divine, surrendering one's will and want peace for all beings. 16 petal lotus.

Ajna the Third Eye Chakra is between the eyebrows, its colour is indigo and mantra OM. It influences the pineal gland, eyes, ears and nose. It is the centre of intuition and insight where we transcend the ego. Through meditation our *third eye* opens and we have deeper states of awareness and realisation. This chakra is blocked by delusions and separation, one may feel egotistical and blame others or God for unpleasant experiences. Physical problems are headaches, eye issues and blindness. When open we have heightened imagination and we receive messages from Divine Intelligence and may experience clairvoyance. 2 petal lotus.

Sahasrara the Crown Chakra on top of the head, its colour is violet and it influences the pituitary gland. It is the centre of Spirituality and Pure Cosmic Energy where feminine Shakti energy unites with the masculine Shiva energy in supra-conscious ecstasy called Samadhi. This is the merging of our *Soul Consciousness with the Cosmic Consciousness of God* where we experience self-realisation, unconditional love and oneness with all things! When open one realises '*I Am Divine*' and vibrates love energy to heal and manifest anything. 1,000 petal lotus.

This is the process of life, to raise the Kundalini up through the chakras working through our life lessons and challenges, dissolving karma and evolving from lower states of ego mind into higher states of soul consciousness which may take one lifetime or many lives. When I was young and unaware I lived mostly externally from my lower three chakras, but as I grow older and wiser external things do not seem to fulfil me any more. Consequently I can feel myself going inwards and thinking and feeling from my higher chakras which heightens my spiritual vibration, heightens my magnetism and therefore heightens my love and attraction. This is the mystical process which is opening the lotus petals of my heart and helping me to see the truth of life!

After all the snow had gone and the bright green forests and vegetable fields reappeared, we experienced a dreadful storm! Our house stood alone at the top of the valley and was completely exposed to the elements. This storm was directly over the top of our house and so strong that, at six in the morning, thunder shook us out of our beds, terrifying the children, and the next round of lightning hit the roof, travelling through the walls to blow up my brother's TV and the tower of my computer! We couldn't afford to buy new ones as all our money had gone on diesel for the radiators and paraffin for the fires to try to keep warm through the terribly cold winter.

As funds were low, the whole family decided to see what treasures we had to sell. I had a lovely hand-carved, gold necklace and some old gold rings, my partner and dad both had heavy gold necklaces and I even found some gold bracelets of the children's that they received from their Italian family when they were born but never wore. We sold it all at the local jewellers who weighed the gold and gave us the money we needed to put food in the two fridges and pay our electricity bill. My mum even sold her mother's gold watch and, even worse, her wedding ring which my dad had saved up for weeks to give her when they got married forty years before!

> "We had reached an all-time low as there was nothing left to sell! However, I did feel at this point of my life I had to lose materially to gain spiritually"

I then promised myself that I would never allow something as bad as my parents nearly dying from carbon monoxide poisoning or having to sell all our gold jewellery, to ever happen again! I knew I must listen to my own inner guidance, making my own decisions and, choices, and that one day I would be spiritual and successful and therefore take care of my family by myself! For I need to fill myself up with love energy and keep it flowing up my spine towards heaven because when creative thoughts in my mind are powered with *feelings from my heart and higher chakras* I create myself, my life and the world around me better than I ever have before.

When I believe in myself and have acceptance, wisdom and persistence to live through my pains and sufferings I know I will be awakened and guided by my spiritual helpers towards my *destiny*. When I go into meditation asking for guidance or what action I need to take, if I am open, I always get answers, inspirations and nudges from my soul which is constantly steering me back towards my true path and spiritual calling. I understand that I must not criticise any situation and the choices I make are never wrong because by learning from them they guide me to make better, higher choices and eventually to choose only love!

It does not matter what life brings me. I believe in my heart that everything will be OK because this is my joy, this is my pain and this is my awakening! In the *fullness of time and if I have patience and faith* I will be given realisation of all I have asked for and I know my children, family and I will have fabulous lives one day – living in appreciation and happiness, not fear and worry. Divine love energy is bringing this to me, as I am purifying and preparing myself and I am thinking higher thoughts, feeling improved emotions and performing enhanced actions which include and embrace all beings. I can sense my amazing life that I am creating in my mind coming to me and when I learn to stay in the love, I will receive it with joy because all I want is to help everyone find peace and self-realisation.

The Buddhists tell us that we can uplift others by truly listening to them; they call this *deep listening!* It's when we allow people to vent their frustrations and react to what they are saying with compassion – even if we disagree with their comments. We can also uplift others by sending love energy to them as this heightens their awareness and, as we give love, we receive love! I told myself that I would try to do this with every person I came into contact with because by giving and receiving prana freely and passing it on to each other, we manifest enlightenment for all beings. For we live in a loving, supportive, abundant universe; we just have to believe and allow ourselves to be in harmony with the flow of

God's love energy that lies within each and every one of us.

> "This is the Age of Aquarius and this is
> the Age of Awareness,
> And this is the Age of Sharing the Love and
> Sharing the Energy"

CHAPTER 6

RELEASING OUR FEARS

Learning to Meditate is the greatest gift you can give yourself in this life. For it is only through meditation that you can undertake the journey to discover your true nature, and so find the stability and confidence you will need to live and die well. Meditation is the road to enlightenment.

SOGYAL RINPOCHE

Our two beautiful sheepdogs are crossed with Alsatian; the male Rio looks like a big black wolf and when the postman drives down to our house he never gets out of his car; instead he beeps the horn for us to come out and collect the post because he's so terrified of them! Yet our dogs are very sweet and, in the eight years we have had them, not once have they growled at the children who would pull their ears and fur. When springtime arrived again, our female dog India came into season. Rio would not leave her alone and we had a little group of neighbours' dogs sniffing around the property. We tried to keep her away from them all, but she became pregnant and eight weeks later she gave birth under the main house to the tiniest, most beautiful puppies that we had ever seen. Eight hungry puppies... *Oh, no, not more mouths to feed!*

We made a quiet bed where their mother could feed them safely and, as they started to grow and open their eyes, they were so cute and cuddly. The puppies would jump with joy and dance with delight all over the children who couldn't get enough of them. Some were black and white, some were black and tan and we gave each one a name. I took photos of the pups and put them all over town in an attempt to try to find them homes, but here in Italy people only wanted small dogs. We started weaning them and they grew so fast with the portions of dog food becoming larger and larger which was costing us a fortune. Their appetites were insatiable; every time we put their food bowls down it became a feeding frenzy and was like a fight for survival. Soon they became too big to keep under the main house so my dad made a large pen under the half-finished house which gave them a big enclosure to run around in.

Our next-door neighbour, who owns the organic cantina which my dad had picked grapes for, is an old, traditional Italian farmer. He keeps lots of animals on his land – chickens, goats, turkeys and rabbits that he would kill and eat, and he even killed the baby goats that his grandchildren played with! We heard that the children came running in from school one lunchtime asking where their baby goats were, but it was too late as they were already on the table being served up for lunch, which in my opinion is horrible. I know that here in the country, farmers need to kill their animals for food if they are poor or if they make a living from them; this I accepted as a normal way of life for them. However our neighbour had an enormous winery that exported wines all over the world and he clearly had lots of money, so why did he need to eat the baby goats?

One morning I went and asked him if he knew of anyone who wanted a puppy and he said to me in Italian which I managed to translate, "You should have drowned them all at birth, then you wouldn't have had a problem now." It really is unbelievable that some people do not have any understanding of how precious all forms of life are, and some of those people are the inhumane hunters in this region of Italy! These hunters are men (if you could call them that) who go around in all their army combat clothes and loaded guns, thinking they can kill any life they want. You always hear their guns going off day and night from miles away because they shoot everything – even the little birds! My daughter's friend from school had the worst experience with them. She and her family had five lovely dogs that were kept on the land surrounding their house which is on the other side of the valley in Ripatransone. They woke up one morning to find all five dogs lying on the ground dead… they had eaten poisoned meat left by the terrible hunters who have no regard for life. These hunters are allowed to walk all over your land with their hound dogs and loaded rifles which really scare my children, and I worry that they might hurt our dogs.

The government has to put a stop to this barbaric so

called 'sport', otherwise there will be no more wildlife left in our area at all. I believe in Peace on Earth for all living beings, not just people! As ethical humans we need to comprehend that being kind and compassionate towards animals helps us to develop kindness and compassion towards each other! I despise any sort of violence which is the way spiritually unconscious people assert themselves to prove that what they are doing is right. Violence and cruelty create more violence and cruelty; once one person is violent to another person they then become violent, taking it out on the next person and onwards it goes; never stopping until it meets with an aware, awakened, spiritual soul who transforms the violence into *love and compassion*.

A couple of weeks later, while I was out shopping in the big supermarket down by the beach, I received a phone call from my mum. She told me that my beloved cat Shui whom we had brought with us from England (and who used to have a brother called Feng) had been run over outside our house. They found him on the roadside, a black and white sleeping beauty so spiritual and intuitive, more like a dog than a cat. I'd had him before the children were born when I lived on my own in London. He was my special friend and would always lie beside me every time I practised yoga and meditation. My partner dug a grave for him on the furthest corner of the land and through our tears the children and I laid flowers inside and said a little prayer. I will always remember my cat with great affection and his passing made me contemplate the mystical subject of death!

In Emmanuel's Book 2 *"The Choice for Love"* it says:

"Dying is absolutely safe. The fear of death is the fear of letting go, The process of dying is always a joyous one, once the human fear has been overcome. When fear is laid aside, death becomes a most exciting adventure. There is nothing to fear in the Universe, Nothing. You have not ceased to exist but have gone into another level of more intense existence"

I have never been afraid to die! Before my children were born I parachuted out of a plane in Austria. I recalled leaping through my fear and diving through the open doorway to free fall through the soft damp clouds, then release my parachute and glide gracefully through the infinite sky until I thankfully touched the ground. I felt such an exhilarating sense of freedom that if I had died at that moment I would have been perfectly happy. It was a daring, fantastic experience; however I only told my parents after I had done it! For I believe with all my heart that our consciousness continues and death is a process of transformation. The Ancient Yogis tell us that the universe is made up of pranic energy and atoms of matter which form Earth, Fire, Water, Air and Ether. In physics we have learnt that neither energy nor matter can be destroyed; they may go through many different transformations, changes and recycling, but they cannot be destroyed. Therefore life which is energy does not cease to exist, life is everlasting and death is an illusion formed from our fearful, egoic minds.

"The truth is; even when we are dead we are still alive! For death is our greatest passage and our grandest awakening"

I remember many years ago when I was travelling around Australia, I lived in a caravan on some farmland close to the Blue Mountains in New South Wales outside of Sydney. When you looked at these magnificent mountains they were actually blue from all the blue leaves growing on the eucalyptus trees which the cute koala bears ate. The farmland was owned by a wonderful old lady called Lynda, who lived in her house alone as her husband had just died a few months before and she had no children. We became great friends, had wonderful talks and I used to cook her dinners and look after her. One day she told me why she believed in life after death. Lynda said that when her beloved father had died of cancer, her mother was distraught so she could not stop crying for weeks and weeks.

One evening she was sleeping in her mother's bed to comfort her and was suddenly woken up in the middle of the night. Lynda looked around and there before her in the corner of the room was her father! He looked young and handsome, except for his feet which were disappearing into the floor. He spoke and told her he loved her, and not to be fearful of death as he was now in the most beautiful garden, surrounded by the most glorious flowers (she told me in life he absolutely adored flowers). Her father said that her mother was grieving far too much for him and holding him back, and could Lynda please tell her mother that it was OK to let him go now. She promised she would and he gave her a big smile and vanished. Lynda told me I was the only other person she told that story to!

Three quarters of the world's population believe in an afterlife of some sort or reincarnation and there have been thousands of case studies documented on people that have died, then been brought back to life with many experiencing a beauteous, peaceful light and *reviewing their life* without judgement. The only important things for them were how loving and forgiving they had been towards others and how much knowledge they had acquired during their time on earth. I know deep in my heart that when we die it is not the end! All the people we have loved and that have died before us will be waiting in the peaceful light with their arms outstretched reassuring us to let go, pass over and feel the majestic, glorious release of death into *God's spiritual world Heaven* which is infinitely more blissful, celestial and melodious than we could ever imagine!

I also believe when our loved ones pass over, we can take comfort in knowing that when we think of them or feel unhappy and distressed, *love* instantly brings their Spirit Soul around us to comfort us – therefore they are only a thought away! I shall help all my loved ones and as many people as I can to realise the truth about death and in their last moments help them to die without fear or judgements, having a smile on their lips in perfect peace!

From *The Prophet* by Kahlil Gibran:

> *"Only when you drink from the river of silence shall you indeed sing. And when you have reached the mountain top, then you shall begin to climb. And when the earth shall claim your limbs, then shall you truly dance. For what is it to die, but to stand naked in the wind and melt into the sun!"*

The puppies were three and a half months old by now and we hadn't found even the smallest one a home! They were quite big and eating normal food, soon it would be either '*we eat or the puppies eat*' – we had to find them homes and fast! My partner advertised them on the internet but had no response. I had to take some action, so without thinking about it first, my brother and I bundled two of them into the car and drove thirty minutes along a lonely country road to the dog pound. We arrived at what looked like a prison camp, an awful place that was packed full of dogs. I rang the bell and the whole pound erupted into a mad barking frenzy with an odd-looking woman coming out to greet us. I explained that we needed her to take the dogs as we could not care for them any more; however she immediately started talking then shouting in very fast Italian which I didn't understand at all. She would not open the gate and kept saying, "No, no, no!" I couldn't believe it, what were we going to do? I was so upset and cried as I looked at the sweet puppies with their big, brown, trusting eyes.

Well back to the car we went, but as I turned the engine on… nothing happened… oh, no, the battery was dead! We were miles from anywhere, beside a quiet road and my phone had no credit! I could see several cars parked inside the pound and had to ring on the doorbell again with jump leads in my hand as we really needed help. I politely asked the woman if she could jump start my car, yet she began shouting and shaking her fists at us. What a horrible woman! She wouldn't help us out, what were we supposed to do? So I kept my finger on the doorbell sending all the dogs into an even greater barking frenzy, and with the dogs in the pound going crazy she began screaming, "Polizia, Polizia." "Yes," I said. "Please call the police, they will help me out!"

My brother and I walked the pups along the winding road until eventually we saw a car and flagged it down. A friendly lady stopped, I asked her for help and she backed her car up without any trouble and jump started my car. At that moment the police arrived – the same two policemen from Ripatransone who had brought my brother home after falling down the cliff, and who had come to my house making sure we had not poisoned my parents! They were not too surprised to see me, yet after talking to the woman from the pound and coming to the conclusion that she was a little crazy, they asked her for her papers! Afterwards, they told me if we wanted to get the puppies taken by the pound we had to go to the town hall, fill in an enormous amount of paperwork and wait for permission before anything else could be done.

There is one thing that is so frustrating in *bella Italia* and that is the awful bureaucracy and red tape you have to go through before anything official can be completed. They must consume thousands of trees in this country for all the paper they use and you need to get permission for everything then sign your life away. Government agencies are the worst; nobody really knows what they are supposed to be doing and if someone who is dealing with your case is not there, the whole thing comes to a standstill. They send you all over town to various office buildings, finally arriving at the last one where they tell you that your letter is in the post and will arrive in two days, but in my experience this is more like two months! It is so time-consuming and they tend to make new rules up as they go along. If you are fortunate enough to know someone in the office, great, you are in; if you cannot speak fluent Italian you're there all day long.

We drove back home with the puppies and emailed everyone trying to find someone to take them and finally found a woman who ran a shelter for animals. My dad and I took four pups down to the shelter for one of her open days, to show them off to people and amazingly they were found homes that very night. In time, the others went to good, loving families with children, and one even went to a vet. We were all very relieved and had our female dog sterilised immediately!

As the days became warmer, the children and I would walk over to my beloved cat's grave and lay down fresh flowers for him. I thought about him often as he had been such a cherished part of our family and we all missed him curling up on our laps in the evenings and nudging us awake in the mornings. Even though I knew when my time came to pass over our souls would be together again, because love never dies, his death affected me. It made me think about my grandmother and grandad who had both died when I was young, and it's strange because up until then I had believed in God! I remember I would pray every night to please keep all my family (I would say each person's name) safe and not let any of them die. But when my grandmother died suddenly and my grandad got sick from cancer and died quickly, I was so upset that I never consciously prayed again until I had my first baby and yoga came into my life! I sort of rejected God and thinking about it now maybe this had something to do with me getting involved with negative people and allowing myself to be used by others.

Subsequently I craved further knowledge on the subject of death and searched my bookcase to find *The Tibetan Book of Living and Dying* by Sogyal Rinpoche which is such an incredible, emotional book. I also found more ancient scriptures on yogic philosophy that tell us: we are celestial souls, not physical bodies; that our body is material, it is temporary and will deteriorate and die, but our soul is spiritual, it is eternal and is never born so can never die. The Spirit Soul resides in the spiritual and physical worlds at the same time, it is the essence of all wisdom and cannot be seen; only experienced. At the moment of death our soul, consciousness which includes our subtle energy bodies, speeds up vibration to separate from the material flesh body and pass over into the spiritual realm, heaven, to become the *Spiritual Body*.

I believe as we die what we think, feel and ask for will be manifested into our reality. If we believe in heaven we may create that to be so or if we believe in hell we may create that to be so until we awaken from the illusion of our minds and return to the place where we were all born from at the beginning of creation, returning home to the oneness, home to divine love and home to paradise. This philosophy touches my heart because I know without a doubt that it is the *Truth!* In all of our wondrous collective creation *there is only God, only Love,* there is no devil, no death, no hell and no judgement or condemnation. The Ancient Yogis tell us that after we pass over, our karmic evolution will determine whether our spiritual body goes back to earth to accept a new material body and create itself again or move on to greater forms of existence or if we are enlightened we do not reincarnate again, but *merge straight into Nirvana!* Through a vision I once had, I vividly saw that as we reach higher states of enlightenment and become a true *God or Goddess* we can move on to other universes, creating our own world out there in the vastness and magic of infinity.

In the Vedic and Buddhist scriptures it is believed there are billions of world systems in our universe, many with the presence of life, and there are different dimensions, realms and worlds within our physical and spiritual skies that we may go to while we are living and when we pass over. Dimensions are different states of consciousness; we are multidimensional beings and our earthly life is lived in the third egoic dimension, but as we evolve our consciousness, we may ascend to the fifth or higher dimensions of unconditional love and God's Heavenly Realms. Consciously evolving higher and higher is a law of nature and to me this process is again represented by the Lotus Flower where its roots are in the dirty water which is ignorance, material craving and the lower dimensions. Then it grows and evolves, raising itself upwards out of the water into the light of the higher dimensions to unfold into the stupendous flower of enlightenment and *become one with the Universe!*

This is also the same in human beings as the Kundalini energy rises up the spine through each chakra, it unites Shakti with Shiva in Samadhi which is our own state of Heaven. Heaven is not a place; it is a higher dimensional state of consciousness that we shift our reality into and it means to have a Divine Life Now! Therefore, as within the macrocosm of God the universe, so it is within the microcosm of the human being and we can all experience enlightenment, heaven, right now, right here on earth, in our physical body and help others achieve the same, until every soul is the representation of love which is Humanity's Ascension where Heaven and Earth join together as one!

> "Our absolute reality is *We Are a Part of God*
> This is the Secret to Eternal Life!"

Once the hot Italian summer arrived with its endless blue skies, it lifted my spirits and I began to feel a lot happier because I loved to be warm and because my body did not like the cold. In the wintertime the central heating in my yoga room never worked properly! During my yoga classes all my muscles would tighten up and my students and I would have to wear cumbersome clothes to stop ourselves from freezing. It was so much better for my body to perform yoga in the warm sunshine and to wear light clothes so I could move into the asanas easily and release the negative energy from my body effortlessly. In England I used to teach yoga in an awesome, heated health club with sauna and steam room. I remember having uplifting times with my girlfriends in the sauna and steam room. Sitting naked, chatting together, sharing experiences and inner thoughts and bonding with the *sacred feminine* within us all. It had been a few years since I'd had a relaxing sauna that sweated out toxins from my body and I knew I would incorporate these health-giving practices into my yoga retreat.

Thinking about my girlfriends made me miss them all terribly, so I called up one of my friends in England and she decided to come over for a little holiday with her daughter. As the building work on the house had not been completed they slept in the same bedroom as my three girls and because it was the height of summer we had all the windows open to try to get some cool evening breeze. In the middle of the night I was suddenly woken up by my eldest daughter Lola running into my bedroom screaming, "Mummy, Mummy quick, there's something on my bed!" I thought she had dreamed it but she was very persistent and, as I slowly got up, I heard my girlfriend scream… I ran into the bedroom, switched all the lights on and to my astonishment saw a big, black fruit bat flying around the ceiling!

Well, all the other girls screamed and ran out of the room, yet me being quite a brave girl who had lived in Australia with all the poisonous creepy crawlies there, had to think of something fast. I thought the bat was cute and didn't want to hurt it so I looked outside and found an old fishing net that we used at the beach to catch crabs in, and very gently caught the bat in the net and put it safely out of the window. I called the girls back inside, but heard more screams and ran into the junk room to see a tiny baby bat circling overhead. The other one must have been its mother who had been looking for it. I opened all the windows and closed the door as that room had been used by the old occupants to hang and dry meat and vegetables with the ceiling open all the way to the roof, too high to reach. Eventually we went back to sleep, although I think my girlfriend and her daughter had a very restless night dreaming of big black bats!

Living in the Italian countryside one gets used to all the fruit bats, lizards and big hairy spiders and insects. In the middle of summer we have to be very careful of snakes and I am always telling the children not to run in the long grass around our land because that's where they like to sleep and lay their eggs. On one exceptionally hot morning I woke up and sleepily went downstairs to make the children's breakfast. As I opened the kitchen cupboard to get the cereals out, there was a baby black snake about thirty centimetres long, hissing at me with its long tongue and trying to bite me. I made a little cry of shock, slammed the cupboard door shut and shouted for my dad who grabbed some rubber gloves, held it by its neck and let it go well away from the house.

A few days later as I was doing the washing-up, I looked out of the window and saw a three-foot long black snake, right outside my kitchen door! I shouted at the children to get inside and they all began yelling at it from the upstairs window trying to make it go away. My big dog Rio growled menacingly at it, but the snake's head just writhed upwards into the air, taunting and provoking him further. Then to our amazement my dad ran over, picked the snake up by the neck and began wrestling with it. The snake got loose from his grip and bit him on the hand! He immediately let it go and my dog barked madly, chasing it away into the bushes, protecting his human family. Black snakes are OK in our area; it's the brown and white ones which are poisonous; however we were all really happy to see my dad alive and well the next day!

Yet we could never kill any animal or insect because

they all have the same *Soul Consciousness* within as we do and as much right to live on Mother Earth as the rest of us! Man kills senselessly because he is scared and fearful, and because of the aggressive, violent uncontrolled pain-body that's inside him. Only by embracing spiritual compassionate values and changing the way we think and feel, can we change ourselves and see the world as a loving, peaceful place. Only then can we hold *every life* in the highest regard and look at killing even an insect as old-fashioned and the wrong way to act!

Facing and releasing our fears, especially our fear of death, helps us have the freedom to change. We all *'Die'* and if we can accept this fact then we can truly begin to *'Live!'* When we understand about the impermanence of life, that all things are created or born, grow and evolve and then decay, wither and pass away, and that everything changes, transforms and recycles into something else; when we cease to be afraid of dying and realise the truth that the physical body dies, but the spirit soul lives on, is eternal and there is no extinction; we become less fearful and develop the courage to be who we truly are in every moment and in all situations.

Releasing our fears means bringing to the surface all those fearful, negative aspects of ourselves that we have been trying to suppress in our pain-body. I saw that my fear of unworthiness, my fear of failure and my fear of not being good enough over the years had been giving off strong vibrations, and by putting my attention on what I feared, I would manifest my fears into my reality. My ego feeds on fear which comes from my memory of past conditionings and hurts. Yet fear cannot exist in the present because the present is a completely new and pure moment of now which is filled with the power of divine love and is not tainted by any negative emotions from my past. When I live in the now I am secure in my truth and peace within, and I do not need, want or fear anything which gives me *true freedom!* I see that fear and negative emotions are all in my egotistical mind; they are just thought waves and thought waves in my mind can be changed because by releasing and embracing my fears they become powerless.

Fear makes everyone feel isolated and insecure and fear takes. However we may conquer our fear by being brave enough to go within and to know that when we are babies we all need love and comfort from others, when we are dying we all need love and comfort from others and when we are living in between birth and death we all need to give and receive love and comfort to each other. The more I practise yoga, meditation and yogic breathing which brings me into the now, and the more faith and belief I have in God, love or a higher power, the more my fear is beginning to dissipate.

Buddha said:

> *"The wisest beings are those who are Fearless, Silent and Loving"*

The yogic breath is a simple exaggeration of our own natural way of breathing. Fear is blocked emotions restricting the flow of pranic energy within and, in times of stress, people hold on to the breath and breathe shallow, using the top lungs only. Breathing yogically uses the lungs at their full capacity and equalises the flow of energy throughout our body. I begin yogic breathing by sitting on the floor with crossed legs or in a chair with a straight back and I close my eyes and breathe myself into presence. Then I take long, slow, deep breaths into my stomach which is the area of the lower lungs and continue breathing into my chest which is the middle lungs, and finally filling my upper chest which is the top lungs. I pause briefly and breathe out slowly in the same order, lower, middle, top, repeating at least ten times. The yogic breath improves vitality, revitalising and bringing fresh prana into every cell of the body. It lessens anxiety and stress, completely relaxes us and helps to develop a calm attitude in life, releasing all fears, especially fear of death.

As I strolled through town looking at other people, I sensed their false destructive fear and negative thoughts and feelings were preventing them from being truly happy or living the lives they wanted to live. I saw the same thing in my parents and I wanted all to understand that by releasing fear and negativity and choosing love and positivity, and most importantly by forgiving ourselves and others, we can change our minds, change our bodies and change our lives. For we need to forgive everybody for everything now and not wait until it's too late!

Cultivating the eternal truth of forgiveness in life is one of the most important spiritual values to acquire, and remembering that everyone does their best with the knowledge that they have at the time helps us to forgive. Reacting with forgiveness and forgiving everyone and ourselves for all of the supposed mistakes, wrongdoings and bitter hurts, frees us from the past and from our fear which naturally makes us feel good. Long-term resentment can have physical effects on our bodies and can show up as migraines, heart attacks and cancer. In our cause and effect universe, when we forgive it goes out along the universal energy field and all of nature absorbs it and returns it to us as *joy*! However in the areas of our lives where we cannot or will not forgive this is a blockage in the flow of our energy, success and happiness; the only way to unblock it is to release the person or situation with forgiveness.

> "Forgiveness means only remembering the loving thoughts, feelings and words we gave to others and that were given to us."

Once we see that there must be a reason for people's behaviour and a reason for the situation we are going through and that even though it has hurt us, this hurt is allowing us to see its purpose in our life, and helping us to understand that when we forgive someone we are not setting them free, we are setting ourselves free!

> "Therefore let us be present and let go of our grievances and resentments,
> Because everything is forgiven in this Divine Moment of Now!
> Because *here* we are fearless,
> Because *here* we begin again,
> And because *here* we never die,
> but live on in Everlasting Bliss"

CHAPTER 7

MY YOGIC DIET

Vegetarian food leaves a deep impression on our nature. If the whole world adopts vegetarianism, it can change the destiny of humankind!

ALBERT EINSTEIN

As we could not secure a mortgage or a personal loan, the only thing to do was to contact our family in England and ask if we could borrow some money to complete the work on the main house, leaving the other house unfinished. We had a great relationship with our family and they seemed to be the only people that could help us. Also my parents and I decided that while Italy is gloriously beautiful and the people are incredibly friendly, it was not the right country for us. The region we lived in was far too cold in the winter, which was not good for my mum's health, and the cost of living was expensive. There were no activities for children to do in our area, people were not into yoga and because I hadn't been able to create my yoga retreat or have spiritual talks with people from all around the world, it was just too quiet for me here in the countryside as the only things passing by our front door were tractors and herds of sheep!

I wanted to walk into town and live in a much livelier, multicultural place because there was not much life happening in Ripatransone! For me, Italy seemed to be an extremely male-dominated society; when going out for lunch you would rarely see women or young children like you do in England. The restaurants, bars and streets were always full of men while all the women were at home in the kitchen cooking up a storm of three-course meals for lunch and dinner. My daughter's teacher often talked about the inequality between men and women in Italy and my partner's step-mamma said to me once, "Italy is a man's country, ruled by men, for men!" Here, most of the men live with their mammas who do everything for them, then when they're around forty years old they decide to marry a young Italian girl who becomes like a surrogate *mamma* and of course does everything for them!

One of my female yoga students refuses to marry or have an Italian boyfriend, preferring English or foreign men who seem to be more liberated and free-thinking. This is the twenty-first century and it should be *equality for all!* Both men and women go out to work these days and both should come home to look after the children, help out with the cooking and share the housework. All of us need to realise that raising children is the most important job in life! We have the responsibility of teaching and guiding the next generation to become caring, kind-hearted beings and for them to join together through peace, love, unity and equality and help heal the world for their children.

As a woman I have come to see that some women have unconditional love in their hearts and are able to express their emotions more easily than men. Consequently I believe there needs to be a lot more women in positions of power to influence, guide and give out love, forgiveness, compassion and acceptance through these times of conflict and adversity which are in our world today. In old indigenous cultures, women had as much power as men. There were great women chiefs and warriors and, in some of today's tribes, women still hold positions of power and make important decisions based on the safety, health, happiness and future of their children and the whole of the tribe. This is so different from our male-dominated society where decisions are based on who is the most powerful, who has the most money and who wins!

I have always helped and empowered women, and I am teaching this to my daughters so they can empower the girls and women they meet in their lives; as the feminine love nature is the only real force in this universe. This is the sacred power that can change the strong aggressive ego in some men and women and therefore change our world because love is not weak! Love is strong and firm and gentle, and the only way to end conflict is by focusing on peace and giving out love. I am also really happy that I had my boy as I feel it is important for us women to teach our boys to respect, cherish and learn from their mothers; so they can grow into wise, nurturing men who are able to give their love unconditionally to the women and children in their lives, and so they can understand that being 'selfish and greedy' or 'taking what's mine' or 'wanting to win' segregates us while being generous, patient, fair and honest brings us all together, making our world a much friendlier, uncompetitive place to live in.

Women and men need to see that life is about *unity* between the sexes not separation, as seeing ourselves as separate from each other is the cause of all our misery. We must celebrate our differences and heal our segregation by opening our hearts to each other and sorting out the problems in our world in a spiritually truthful, collectively loving, unifying way that includes all nations and gives all people the basic *right to a decent life.* For there is only *one race* of people on Mother Earth and it is the *Divine Human Race which seeks peace and democracy for all.* That's why I want my children to grow up on a yoga retreat so they can be surrounded by nature, truth and spiritual freedom.

We thought about opening our retreat in the south of Italy where it was warmer, but the children's nonno said there was far too much 'mafia' in that region and we wouldn't like it. Also, while the Italian fish restaurants by the sea are incredibly delicious, the restaurants in Ripatransone were meat-based and seemed to serve the same bland pasta dishes. We missed going out for dinner to Indian, Thai, Chinese and Japanese restaurants; there was only one average Chinese in San Benedetto and the only takeaway food anywhere was pizza! Thai or Indian food products were difficult to find in the shops so we had to rely on our family and friends sending the spices over by post. If we lived in Rome or closer to a city we would find these restaurants; but it would be too expensive for us to make our retreat there. In England we'd always go out for dinner or have a takeaway at least once a week, but in Italy I seemed to be cooking all the time – oh how lovely it would be to get dressed up and go out for a fragrant Thai dinner that drove my taste buds wild!

There are no vegetarian restaurants in our area and only one health food shop which is expensive. I found it almost impossible to find health foods in the supermarkets and they were only just introducing wholemeal pasta, bread and flour. Also there was not much variety in the vegetables, although the tomatoes, baby oranges and fruit were the best I had eaten!

Over the years, while practising yoga, my body has become lighter and so gradually my food needs have become lighter too – I never eat meat, but I do eat a little fish or seafood once or twice a month. Most people will say they need to eat meat to get protein; however this is incorrect as we get protein in plants and in many other foods, and our bodies only require ten per cent of protein a day. Vegetarians have lower cholesterol and fewer heart problems; they are less likely to suffer from constipation, high blood pressure, diabetes, obesity or food poisoning.

There are many documentaries online such as *A Delicate Balance, The Truth,* showing us how scientists and doctors have proven that vegetable proteins are more efficiently used by the human body than animal proteins, and that eating fat and protein from animals and dairy sources may cause and enhance cancer, heart disease, diabetes and many other illnesses while eating a vegetarian/vegan wholegrain plant-based diet, with fewer or no animal products, prevents and reduces them. They also tell us the structure of our teeth and digestive system are not designed for eating meat and that the human digestive tract is twelve times as long as our body for the long digestion of plants. In carnivorous animals their teeth are sharp in front and designed for meat eating and they have a short digestive tract, only three times the length of their body, to expel meat quickly so it does not poison the system.

Leo Tolstoy told us:

> *"If a man earnestly seeks a righteous life*
> *His first act of abstinence is from animal food!"*

Yogis are vegetarians, and they believe in non-injury to all living beings, animals and the earth. When we eat meat all the pain-energy of the dying animal remains inside its muscles and is taken into our bodies, making our emotions increasingly difficult to control. Every week two billion animals are slaughtered and eaten; most of the grain the world grows is given to livestock to make meat instead of feeding starving people and the destruction of our sacred rainforests by cattle farmers is reducing the world's oxygen at an alarming rate! The animal agricultural industry causes fifty per cent more greenhouse emissions than world transport and uses up seventy per cent of all water resources. This industry is affecting our oceans with ninety per cent of small fish ground up to be made into pellets to feed even more livestock and overfishing from the fishing industry is killing off our coral reefs and delicate ecosystems, and depleting our oceans at an unsustainable rate. Five hectares of land is needed to grow food for each person eating a meat-based diet while five hectares of an organic soya crop would provide the most energy and feed thirty people. The UN has urged a *global shift* towards vegetarianism and veganism to save the world from hunger, fuel poverty and the worst impacts of climate change in our very near future.

Man thinks he is an advanced race, but each year all nations jointly spend trillions of dollars on war and nuclear arms while 30,000 people (mainly children) *die of starvation a day*. Surely the preservation of '*Life*' is far more important than building missiles and nuclear bombs! If we had peace and unity this money could be used to feed, clothe and care for each and every one of us! Mother Earth has enough natural resources and abundance to feed all the people on earth, yet lack of proper distribution to the people who really need it causes them to starve, while prosperous countries throw away enough food every day to feed the entire planet! Instead of thinking in an egotistical, selfish way by individually holding on to resources, wealth and food which many people with money and power are doing, we awakening individuals must join together, using the power of the people to collectively discover new ways to use our technologies so that we can distribute resources, wealth and food conscientiously and give *all* human beings an opportunity for a more joyful existence.

Let us remember that we are all the same, we are human/spiritual beings who want to be happy and that being human and being spiritual is what we all have in common; it's our mutually dependent nature and our Divine Connection. Thus nurturing all people and every species on our planet is a way of nurturing ourselves! Understanding this is true *spiritual advancement* which can only come about by having peace within oneself then sharing peace with others.

Subsequently I began to see that I wanted to open my retreat in a much more spiritually free and livelier environment, as the only way to survive or have any kind of social life in such a small town as Ripatransone was to become an Italian. To have a siesta when everyone else does, to have a late dinner at the same time they do and to send the children to a Catholic school, but I didn't want to become an Italian as I did not feel that Italy was my true home. I didn't even feel like I was a true English person either; I considered myself a *citizen and natural person of the Earth* and needed to be around all types of people from every walk of life. My family and I decided that we wanted to live in a warmer climate and open our retreat where there would be many more Europeans and people from all different countries who were more into yoga. So we decided on Andalusia in Spain with its amazing beaches, stunning mountains and much more affordable houses.

We researched the area thoroughly on the internet to find lots of activities for the children to do with animal, marine and wildlife parks and best of all there were over sixty different restaurants from all around the world!

Also when we were younger my dad had a boat moored in one of the pretty marinas and we spent many holidays there and had family living in that area for over twenty years. We could buy a large plot of 'flat' land close to the sea with two houses, wooden chalets for our yoga guests and a large swimming pool and yoga room. I had a vision of my dream and drew a picture of my retreat which I put on my kitchen wall so every day I could look upon it and ingrain the image into my mind.

At that time I read one of the most inspirational books, *You Can Heal Your Life* by Louise Hay. She believes that there are mental causes for physical diseases, telling us "if you change the way you think, you can change your life" and "what you give out in life, you get back!" which is the same philosophy as yogic karmic beliefs and divine law. Seventy per cent of our thoughts are negative and limit our powers, so by changing them it helps us to feel good and when we feel good we give off good vibrations and attract positive things into our lives. We can help to create our spiritual and material goals with *affirmations and confirmations* which are positive intentions we write down or say out loud to ourselves every day; they build our self-esteem and our self-love and get us into our feel-good place! These autosuggestions influence our subconscious mind and, when mixed with positive feelings of faith and visualisation, they disperse negative thoughts, change our beliefs and eventually manifest into their physical equivalent.

I started writing and vocalising my affirmations and confirmations daily as they helped to focus my mind on the things I loved and on the kind, loving person I wanted to be. I knew I had to repeat them in present time, in the here and now because if I said *'I want'*, *I would be wanting forever!* I kept writing these affirmations "I am so thankful that I feel good, I feel love and I feel joy now" and "I am so thankful that my house is complete now". I did things that brought me into my feel-good place and I visualised my house looking perfect and I totally believed it.

Our family in England then lent us the money to complete our house, thank goodness! We could not afford to pay professionals so we did all the work ourselves which was an enormous undertaking. I repainted the bedrooms upstairs and my parents put in a new bathroom with all the plumbing downstairs. As the weather was good my dad and I had the overwhelming task of repainting the whole outside of the house! Firstly we rendered the lower walls, then to paint the house we had to build three levels of scaffolding, one on top of the other, and fix a ladder onto the third level to paint the highest point; it was so high that when the wind came up it would sway. My dad hates ladders and had to have a glass of red wine which gave him the courage to climb up to the top! I painted the lower half of the house and eventually we finished it, laying pathways of shingle and logs to finish the outside. The white paint was so bright in the dazzling Italian sunshine you had to wear sunglasses to look at it!

Meanwhile, the bar where my partner worked had closed down, so with time on his hands he created an amazing false ceiling in the kitchen as he had done some work as a dry liner before in England. He was having trouble finding another job as there was not much call for a cocktail barman in our sleepy region of Italy. Consequently he collected the dole for the first time in his life which only lasts for eight months in Italy and only if you have worked before for two years; after that, there's no more help from the Italian government. If a woman is unmarried, has not worked and wants to leave her partner for any reason or if her partner leaves her and she is left on her own with children to support she receives no money from the government and has to fend for herself or rely on her own family if she has any or, as a last resort, go to the Catholic Church for help!

My partner searched the internet for jobs and emailed all his friends. One friend was working in Marbella, Spain and earning lots of money. He decided he should try for a job there and he booked his plane ticket, packed his bags and the children and I saw him off!

After he left, my parents and I began creating a large en suite wet room off my daughter's bedroom with mosaic tiles that would look elegant and stylish. My dad and I carried about forty boxes of very heavy tiles into the hallway from outside and the next day my forearms hurt so badly I could barely hold my knife and fork! I have never had any fear of hard work and I have always been a strong woman. When I was younger I used to go to work with my dad in his metal factory on Saturday mornings and he showed me in his own way to never feel inferior in the company of any man as men and women are equal. I could appreciate this insight a lot more now because deep in my soul I felt I was both feminine and masculine!

In the stupendous book *The Bhagavad-Gita* it tells us that our Spirit Soul is androgynous! Every soul has experienced both sexes in hundreds of previous lives which is the eternal cycle of reincarnation upon the *cosmic wheel* called Samsara in Sanskrit where all beings are subject to birth, death and rebirth. This is the cycle of karma that keeps creating, evolving and dissolving creation, and only when we realise our identity with the Divine, our identity with love, do we revolve upon the wheel no more, and move straight on to the higher dimensions and realms. In other philosophies I have studied it tells us that the soul comes to the earth plane to fulfil its desires and work out its karma and that we have our own soul groups which guide us to fulfil our spiritual purpose. They also tell us that no life is ever wasted or misused as every so-called evil or lazy person is on their own evolutional path; every individual has its own inner work to do and every soul will eventually become *'Enlightened!'*

For the soul must experience many different lives, personalities, thoughts and feelings from the lowest level of consciousness to the highest so it can raise the Kundalini energy up the spine, so it can raise its awareness and transform the *Human Being into a Divine Being!*

I could feel my yogic lifestyle raising my awareness and I found that I didn't want to eat fish or seafood any longer; thus I became a true vegetarian! The yogic diet is based on the *Three Gunas* which, according to the Ancient Yogis, are the three basic material qualities of nature that each individual is conditioned by. They are

Sattva which is goodness, *Rajas* which is material desire and *Tamas* which is ignorance. Tamasic food is stale, fermented and overripe; it does not release life-force energy into the system and affects the body's resistance to disease. Tamasic foods include meat, alcohol and tobacco. Rajasic food is very hot, bitter, sour and salty and will over-stimulate the body. Rajasic foods are too much salt, chocolate, tea, coffee and very hot chilli. Sattvic food nourishes the body and calms the mind.

My yogic vegetarian diet is Sattvic. It consists of wholemeal rice, grains, cereals, pasta, pulses and beans and dried fruits, nuts, seeds, herbs and honey. I eat lots of organic fresh fruit and vegetables that are in season. I create natural, freshly-made fruit/vegetable, seed/nut smoothies with green super-leaf powder and every day I enjoy a large, raw salad or vegetables which are good for my digestion. I only consume eggs in my cakes that I bake myself with various flours. I eat a little cheese, but mostly enjoy organic tofu, seitan, Quorn and soya products with no GMOs. I drink herbal teas, rice, soy or almond milk and of course lots of natural water which hydrates the whole body, keeping the wrinkles away and helps one to remain youthful. I eat the most watery foods first like fruit, vegetables and salads as they are quick to digest, then I eat my carbohydrates and then proteins as proteins take longer to digest. If I eat them all together the fruit, vegetables and salads will ferment in the stomach which causes bad digestive problems. I also take a multivitamin and B12 now I am a vegetarian.

While cooking I try to be aware and present and give love energy vibrations to the food that I am preparing.

I bless, offer and thank Spirit for my vegetarian food and water as this *spiritualises* it, making it taste infinitely more delicious and giving us health and vitality. I steam or cook my food lightly, eating fresh every day, and try not to have many distractions while eating, although this is sometimes difficult with four children! It has been proven that eating less gives you a longer, healthier life. The amount of food eaten should be the equivalent of two handfuls, no more, otherwise the stomach will expand and begin to want more; therefore don't overload the digestive system and feel too full. It is vital to eat slowly, chewing each mouthful at least twenty-five times with awareness and pleasure which releases the prana in the food and masticates it into a liquid before it goes into the stomach.

My Guru says it's important not to drink large amounts with meals, as liquid puts the gastric fires out and causes bad digestion. Many problems and illnesses within the body are due to dehydration so it's important to drink lots of water between meals as our bodies are made up of seventy per cent water. Drink a big glass of water when you get up which activates the internal organs, lots during the day and one glass of water just before you go to bed to avoid strokes and heart attacks.

My body functions better on this diet; if I have a day of eating processed or chemical-filled foods they will not agree with me, my body will not function properly, feeling heavy, bloated and sluggish and I will have negative thoughts. If we eat unwholesome, incompatible foods they accumulate and clog up the large intestine, becoming undigested and unabsorbed, and can stay in the system for years. When these foods begin to ferment they give off toxins which affect the heat-energy of our digestion, blocking the free flow of energy and causing imbalance within the body, weakness in the internal organs and stressing out the mind. Sun-ripened fruits and vegetables have massive amounts of pranic energy inside of them; they are live foods and full of goodness with the energy of the moon helping our fruits and vegetables taste delicious. The food we eat builds our mind, body and soul so it should be pure, wholesome and nutritious.

> "Food is medicine and eating is a meditation
> Therefore let us respect our bodies and eat to live a healthy life!"

Once all the jobs on the house were finished we called four estate agents who came around and took some lovely photos. They told us the house and land were beautiful and spacious but it was not a good time to sell as the property market was quiet all over Europe and not moving at all. We didn't care what they said; after all our hard work and challenging experiences we were so happy to finally have the property up for sale, it put big smiles on all our faces and we all hoped it would sell as soon as possible. I began writing another affirmation "I am so thankful that my house is now sold and I am living on my yoga retreat in Spain". I visualised and meditated on the picture I had drawn of my retreat and hoped it would be manifested soon.

We had been doing so much work on the house, I felt we needed a break and to give the children some fun. So as it was my son's birthday I decided to take all four children to the zoo in Rome. We boarded the early morning bus which took nearly four hours and made it without causing too much trouble as I did have lots of food, drinks, healthy sweets and books to keep them occupied. Nonno picked us up at the bus station and checked us into a little hotel to the children's delight then he took us on a fantastic sightseeing trip all over the magnificent city of Rome.

First we walked around the colossal, intimidating walls of the ancient Colosseum and just touching it I could sense the amazing history it had witnessed. Then we sauntered through the Forum, the old centre of Rome with its aged political buildings and dusty shrines, and taking shelter from the sunshine we visited the majestic Pantheon which is one of the oldest, most beautiful intact temples in the world! As I stepped inside, my breath was taken away by its incredible domed roof and, making my way through the cool, slightly damp-smelling air to the hole in the centre, sunlight streamed down upon me and I experienced the same connection with the Gods above that the Ancient Romans must have felt a thousand years before!

Although our feet were starting to hurt we carried on through the winding, cobbled streets to the enchanting Trevi Fountain where the children threw coins into its cascading waters and made lots of wishes; then we had a delicious lunch with cake, fulfilling a little dream! The next day we visited the zoo which was lovely and tropical and the children had a great time coming face to face with a large bear through thickened glass. That evening we took the 9pm bus back home which broke down in the mountains. While waiting two hours for another bus to come and rescue us, my children ran up and down the aisles, making new friends until finally exhausting themselves out and falling asleep. Eventually a couple of Italian gentlemen helped to carry my sleeping children one by one over to the new bus and we arrived home in the middle of the night!

While my partner was in Spain, I felt empowered to be on my own. I was having a brilliant time with the children, I could do what I wanted and it was great not to have to cook big Italian dinners. I couldn't afford to buy all the delicious health foods that I needed to make my body feel good so I decided to have one whole day of fasting on fruit smoothies every two weeks. Yoga advises us to eat fruit for one whole day once a month or a smoothie/juice fast which gives the digestive system a much needed rest. It detoxifies us, fights disease and gives us deeper states of awareness. I also began detoxing my body with special yogic techniques called Shat Karmas which are incredible health practices that cleanse the whole body of waste products and toxins. I felt purer and sensed that the fasting and detoxing was changing me profoundly!

As I was getting older, I had been worrying about wrinkles on my face and one morning I woke up with a spiritually guided thought in my mind… to use *Urine Therapy* on my skin! The Ancient Yogis talk about it in all the sacred scriptures and in India it's called 'Amaroli' and used widely. I remembered one of my yoga students in England used it for his cancerous growth with fantastic results and many people who ingest it have cured themselves of illness. I researched this unusual subject on the internet and read a brilliant book called *Your Own Perfect Medicine* by Martha M. Christy. I already knew that urine is not a waste product, it is a by-product of the blood and purified by the kidneys. I found out it has all the nutrients, vitamins and minerals of blood, that it contains our own antibodies which fight disease and it's wonderful for wrinkles!

A previous prime minister of India used it on his face and had soft line-free skin well into his nineties. Consequently I began massaging it into my face every morning and on the dry skin of my body and found because of my healthy yogic diet when used immediately it was odourless. A few months later my wrinkles seemed less prominent and my skin was soft and smooth. I used it on any blemishes, bites or burns and for relieving the children's painful earaches. The big pharmaceutical companies understand the benefits of urine and use a by-product of it called urea in many expensive skin creams. But they will not inform the public because when people begin using their own *free natural medicine* and not the damaging chemical drugs these companies produce, they will all go out of business!

For me, true beauty and health comes from how we think and feel about ourselves, from what we put inside our bodies and from practising yoga and meditation. It is a well-known fact that our bodies get better the more they are used as inactivity dulls the mind and deadens the muscles. If we eat nature's energy-ripened fruits and vegetables, if we keep our bodies and minds strong, fit and free of negativity and most importantly if we love ourselves and give love out to others, we will be happy and the happier we are the healthier and more beautiful we become.

The Dalai Lama tells us:

"Happiness is the highest form of health!"

At that time my yoga classes were trailing off a little, yet even if no one turned up for class I loved it as I could do my beloved Kundalini meditations which were raising the energy up to the higher chakras and bringing me ever closer to my Divine Self. In England my classes were always full; however here students never came regularly and it didn't help with what I read in one of the Italian newspapers. Inside there was a large photo of a woman performing a yoga asana and another of a woman having a shiatsu massage with a picture of the devil next to them! Apparently some priest from a small, rural town in Italy said that yoga and shiatsu massage both let the devil in! I could not believe it when my English girlfriend read the article to me. It is absolutely ridiculous that in this age people are led to believe such rubbish; the priest should have talked to a Sat Guru first and found out the true meaning of yoga before poisoning people's minds.

There is only God, only Love in this universe and God talks to us through our truthful thoughts, feelings and experiences. The devil and hell do not exist; they were made up by early patriarchal fear-worshipping religions where the masculine put the fear of God into us so the masses would separate and be easier to control. Long before them were matriarchal love-worshipping religions of the Goddess, Mother Earth and Nature where the feminine was in control and people lived in peace, love and unity. Evil is produced from the wrong fear-based thoughts and feelings of the unfulfilled, deluded mind and pain-body which creates our words and actions. It causes us and others to suffer and to feel separation from the *divine love within us all*. In every moment we have the choice to express the evil that resides in our egoic minds, therefore choosing fear, or to express the good that resides in our heart and soul, therefore choosing love!

We have the choice to choose between the Yin and Yang, between the different dualities of being happy or sad, truth or delusion, freedom or pain and good or evil which all amounts to the choice between God and the Ego. We have the choice to be our true self without ego now and we have the choice to live in the *'heaven'* that we have created for ourselves here on earth or to live in the so-called *'hell'* that we have created here on earth. In this divine moment we can change our lives; it's our choice and free will to do this and thus attract our own destinies. All of us need to realise that we are spiritual souls having a human experience and our short time on this planet is an exceptional chance to *Give and Receive Love which is the purpose of life!*

Jesus said:

"Give and it shall be given unto you."

In nearly every spiritual book I have read they tell us that giving and receiving are natural forms of karma, attraction and love. Every action of giving will automatically cause its opposite reaction of receiving because everything affects everything else in our cause and effect universe and *because we are all one!* When I feel good I am connected to Spirit and I give joyfully, thereby allowing space for receiving. When I give without wanting something in return, I place myself in the flow of love energy which goes out along the universal energy field affecting others, then my magnetism draws it back to me. But if I am more concerned about the outcome of my giving, this blocks the flow of energy and neither I nor the other person benefits. The ego personality takes and to take is an old, outdated belief, whereas the true self gives and to give is the new current belief! Thus giving is receiving and we must *'give all to receive all!'*

> "Whenever we give from our hearts we receive.
> Therefore let us give to all people, and receive
> our heart's desire."

Divine love/light energy is shared by all beings. It builds up in our soul's aura, vibrating through our open chakras and allows us, through the expression of blissful thoughts, feelings, words and actions, to *give unconditionally*. As this pranic life-force energy increases between people, it magnifies and flows out, causing more of the same love energy. This continuous giving and receiving of energy will evolve humanity's consciousness into a new spiritual awareness which will eliminate evil, greed and distrust in the world, and be the cause of a *New Loving Human Race*!

> "Giving is the New Teaching that will set us all Free."

CHAPTER 8

THE MEANING OF LOVE

*Love is the Divine Essence of who we truly are and as we allow
this essence to flow through us we bring the love back into our
lives which gives healing to others through a smile, a cuddle,
a kind thought, word or act of kindness. It's when we open
our hearts with empathy, truthfulness and forgiveness without
judgement that helps to develop life's purpose; Evolution for
All! This is the New Consciousness of the Heart and the New
Love Awareness which is emerging throughout humanity at this
time and bringing a New Unity and Equality into our world.
For if we think love, feel love and choose love –
it will come to be!*

JOANNE LEE PHILPOT

Each and every one of us are given ideas, messages, coincidences and guidance from our Soul, Spirit Guides, Angels, other people and the natural world around us. I remember waking up one morning quite a while ago with one single powerful thought in my mind… to write this book! Spiritual inspiration began flowing through me and it was so intense, so dynamic that I could not put my pen down. I believe I received this inspiration while sleeping because in this state our soul vibrates out of the body into the spiritual world to rejuvenate and to learn and remember things. Also through raising the Kundalini and heightening my vibration, messages, coincidences and guidance were beginning to accelerate, and I knew I had to pay attention to them as they show me there is always a deeper meaning and a higher reason for what is going on in my life.

We are all awakening and when going through challenging situations and asking: "Why is this happening to me or what have I done to deserve this?" only later do we realise that these were the lessons and desires of previous karma that we had to go through so we could cultivate wisdom and love. In the end it was for the best because when we experience the things we do not want to be, it makes us ask and be thankful for the enriched things that we do want to be! I sensed I was learning all these truths because I was gaining self-control and self-discipline and because I was not being consumed by my chaotic relationship any longer!

It was October and my partner called to say he would be coming home from Spain in a couple of weeks. The children were really missing him; however I seemed not to have missed him at all! Our house was so much calmer and organised without him. My time alone was for doing yoga, Kriya meditations, studying spiritual books and watching life-enhancing movies or documentaries on the internet, but not television as I did not want to fill my head with mind-numbing negativity. I started to limit myself from outside negativity which happened quite naturally as I couldn't afford to pay Sky TV! I rarely watched the news or read the newspapers as they only reported on the *negative, bad things in the world which there is a lot less of, never on the positive, good things in the world which there is a lot more of* – this then causes people to think the world is a bad, evil place with everyone out for themselves.

Watching television is addictive; it makes our younger generation stupid and the older ones spiritually unconscious. Viewing horror and negative images on TV affects the mind and adds to the pain-body. It subjects our children to thousands of simulated murders in their tender years which influences them and may lead to aggressive, dysfunctional behaviour. The more we surround ourselves in this negativity, the more we begin to accept it and think of it as the normal behaviour of people; but this is not true because the basic nature of humanity is good and kind, and the world is getting better, not worse!

When more people believe that there is *only love in the universe,* negative, evil things will begin leaving our existence and bad, misguided people will become spiritually awakened and have compassion for others. Many people derive all their information and all their beliefs from mainstream TV, the media and the newspapers which are filtered, controlled and condition us to stay in our unconscious sleep and not to think for ourselves. Advertising on TV fuels the selfish ego to want more material things and consumerism has taken us over. As the big wealthy corporations create more needs so that we constantly buy more stuff to fill our emptiness which gives us the illusion of happiness and disguises our lack of meaning that we are all searching for!

Yet television, media, film, the internet and radio can be incredible vehicles to put heightened, evolving messages across as they reach all corners of our globe! I believe as humanity's consciousness evolves they will become a lot more spiritually inspiring and educational. They will retain a worldwide responsibility to show and enhance ethical human values and, when used in awareness, they can be vehicles which include not separate humanity, giving unity to all. This is already happening on the internet with real news and spiritual TV channels, and there is a whole subculture of awakening beings emerging and wanting to heal others and share their experiences online.

Thus, let us stop filling our minds with negative images and our houses with more things and let us go outdoors sitting in an inspiring place, being quiet and listening to the birds sing, the wind in the trees or the breath of the ocean. As we do this we make space to communicate with our soul which gives us messages, guidance and peace.

In a few days my partner was arriving back from Spain, but I was apprehensive about him disrupting my peace and tranquillity and for quite a while I had been feeling very unhappy in the relationship. We'd been together for ten years and there had been many special times; however now I was sensing that I had outgrown him, and was not in love any more. I felt we were not good for one another, as we didn't seem to cherish or enrich each other or want the same things in life, and I thought he was not helping me to spiritually evolve. My partner is younger than me and likes to watch violent cage fighting and boxing on the computer which I was forever telling him to turn off as I did not want the children to be affected by it. He still wants to go out with his friends all night long, he still needs to prove himself and like a lot of us women and men he has a large ego.

All of us have forgotten about the Divine Self within and because of this ignorance we have created the separate ego personality which accepts the physical body and chaotic, uncontrolled thinking mind as oneself. We must remember that we are a Spiritual Soul, not this impermanent body or the negative, egotistical mind and its judgemental thoughts. Once we become aware of the false taking ego, we move into alignment with our true giving selves, we know that we are part of the same Soul Consciousness and thus we become a spiritual channel for love to express itself in the world which reconnects us to each other. For our soul within is infinite and everlasting and has far greater power and influence than anything in the outside world which is transient and fleeting.

I felt my partner's ego was a big problem for him; it was coming between us as a couple, getting in the way of his true self and holding him back in life. I tried telling him many times in my own way but he only wanted to listen to himself; he thought he was right about everything and didn't need help or guidance from anyone! I really hoped this time apart had somehow helped him to see his truth and that maybe we could save our relationship and fall in love again! When my partner arrived home the children were ecstatic to see him; he had bought them Spanish flamenco dolls and had lost a stone in weight, looking amazingly handsome. That night we put the children to bed with my parents looking after them and went out to dinner. We had a great time, talking and laughing and he seemed to have genuinely missed me. He was very loving and we jumped into bed as soon as we got home as it had been three months since we had last seen each other.

The next evening I went to bed early as usual as I have to wake up at 6.30am to get the children off to school. I believe not only are my Angels and Guides waking me up spiritually they woke me up that night at 3am to change my life forever! All the children were sleeping, yet I had a strong desire to go downstairs which I never normally do unless I need something from the kitchen. My partner was on the computer as usual in the middle of the night, but as I crept silently down, still half asleep, I could tell by his voice he was not speaking to a male friend…

I was still and silent sitting on the stairs until I heard the words "Baby, what are we going do? I don't want to break anybody's heart here!"… My blood ran cold and my heart pumped loudly inside my chest. I looked around the stairs without him seeing me and there he was with wine in hand, microphone in the other, on Skype, the video phone, 'talking' to some naked girl who was in full view on the screen – obviously his lover… Oh my goodness, what a shock! Anger raced through my veins which propelled me to run up to him and scream in his face, "What's going on!" He quickly switched the computer off and started rambling on about how he was 'in love' with some girl in Spain and that it was my fault that it had happened because I had not been putting him first, and he could not handle being around my parents – basically lots of nonsense that he believed to make himself feel better.

I had so many furious thoughts whirling around inside my head. I could feel the negative emotions trembling through my body, my legs went wobbly and I felt instant fear at the thought of being alone with four children. But then as I sat in a chair I calmed down and began feeling a sublime sense of serenity because I knew at that point our relationship was finally over, and deep in my heart I was secretly relieved! We talked long into the night, holding each other and mourning for the loss of our love. Yet it wasn't me that I was thinking of or worried about; it was the children, as they were so young and I thought they needed their father. Although my partner had been a good provider most of the time, he was not a big outdoor man and didn't play with the children much. In fact he had not been a very good father or husband at all, preferring to be on the computer, watching TV or sleeping off a hangover in the years I had been with him!

The next few days were awful; my whole world had been turned upside down! It was like living in a bad dream! I felt such resentment towards my partner, I couldn't stand being around him any more and I had to get him out of the house. I told him to leave, so he packed his bags and I drove him to his friend's apartment an hour away. As I dropped him off I screeched the car away with tyres blazing and held up two fingers at his astonished face! Not very yogic I know but I was extremely angry.

Our situation was not good, we had no money, my partner had no job and the bills were coming in. He had to come back home after five days and go on the internet to find a job. I hated having him in the house; he was angry and moody all the time. One evening I confronted him and told him that I had never felt so let down in my entire life. Here we were living through all these difficult situations, no work, no money with four children, in a foreign country and he tells me he's in love with some girl. I mean, come on; *what else did I need to go through*! He said he wasn't going to tell me of his affair until he had a good job which would have been worse – living a lie to us all. A few days later he came to me saying, "I'm very confused, I don't even know if I love this girl." I could not believe it, yet for me the damage had been done. We decided the best thing for him to do was to go to London and get a job as he knew lots of people there and could stay at his best friend's house. When I dropped him off at the bus stop I felt so relieved because all I wanted was to be alone!

I believe that a man who needs to have sex with other women when he has a beautiful wife and children at home is a man who has lost his honourable self, is totally consumed by his selfish ego and needs to live his life on his own. My partner had been taking his pleasure and gratifying his lower senses, not caring about whom he hurt or the consequences of his actions! If he treats other women this way he will find it difficult to have a meaningful, loving relationship in life and end up unhappy and alone. It is not morally good to lie and cheat to your family. The choices he is making are creating negative experiences for him in the future and if our girls found out it could influence them in trusting men because it's not a good example for a father of four to set. I felt incredibly hurt, lonely and abandoned, living in this rural Italian countryside and I retreated further into my meditations and began contemplating the *meaning of love!*

For me 'True Love' is when people love and respect each other so much that they do not need to go out and have sex with other people. They have a connection of the heart, mind and soul, and are committed to each other for however long their love lasts! People can say "I Love You" so easily, yet sometimes this is needy fulfilment and emotional attachment which create dependency and obsessive behaviour in relationships because people are not *being their true selves*. They are playing a role and are consciously or unconsciously pretending to be that perfect person to fall in love with, or they are playing games and seeking their negative desires, not from their husbands, wives and partners, but dishonestly behind their backs from other people. However this is not living love's reality, this is living a lie! For love is limitless! Love is truth, freedom, joy and trust, and love is giving as it does not want or need anything from anyone.

> "We cannot truly love if we come from our minds and are fearful. We must come from our hearts and be loving."

Love is Union, the Ego is Separation. Love brings two souls together while the ego pulls them further apart and a relationship based on Ego-Fear, not on Spirit-Love is always wrong, as fear means there can be a lack of love and that love must be possessed or owned; thus a marriage based on selfish reasons or where the man is in control is fearful, not loving. For the ego deludes us all. It makes people stay together because they think the other person can somehow complete them or they feel guilty about the things they did to each other or because they need financial security or they fear loneliness or its a Karmic relationship and they are working out their Karma together.

Yet they are not expressing true love to each other because they do not have a truthful communion of their hearts, minds and souls. They only connect on a physical level and through the ego's negative feelings of guilt and sacrifice which have been substituted for love and honesty, and which precariously holds their dysfunctional relationship together. They are *'in love'* with the illusion of each other which ultimately leads to resentment, blame and suffering, as they will never forgive each other or let each other go and are destined to live a quiet life of desperation and hindrance to self-realisation which causes them to feel even more guilt, pain and fear; until the powers that be intervene by creating an experience that awakens them and sets them both free to grow, evolve and truly love again.

My partner had been in London for a few months and I suppose being on his own in the freezing cold snow made him think about us all. He called me up, saying he loved me, how he wanted us to grow old together and that he missed the children terribly, wanting his family. I felt sorry for him and I told him I loved him and meant it. However, on Christmas evening I was really depressed as we see no one at this time of year and it's always so quiet. I was compelled to go on the computer and somehow managed to access my partner's Facebook site and read all of his personal emails... *Wow, what a shock*! I felt physically sick; there were so many emails from so many girls. I read one from his 'secret lover' in Spain, a different girl from the one I had caught him with on Skype and another from a Romanian girl who called him 'my Italian devil'. They talked about their wonderful summer affair together which had happened in Italy while I was still 'happily' living with him in our house!

I felt absolutely terrible! My partner had been having so many affairs secretly behind my back it hurt me enormously. My heart sank, all my memories of our life together tainted, all a lie. I would have had some respect for him if he had come and told me the first time it had happened but no, he was not man enough for the truth!

I put my coat on and walked along the cold, dark road to the cantina next door to buy a bottle of their superb organic red wine. The owner's son wished me 'Buon Natale' and insisted on giving me the wine for free; I returned his kindness with a weak smile. On the way back I looked up at the stars and with tears welling in my eyes then falling down my cheeks, I begged my Angels to please help me as I had never felt so lost and helpless in my life! When I got home, as it was Christmas, I had a glass of wine with my parents and my dad made us all laugh. After I put the children to bed I went downstairs and poured myself another much-needed glass of wine, then I called up some of my girlfriends in England to wish them a Merry Christmas and tell them about the emails. They were angry at the way my partner had treated me and said it was for the best that my relationship was over and they all told me they loved me.

As I sat quietly stroking my mum's cat that had jumped onto my lap to comfort me, I laid out my Tarot cards and they gave me an important realisation! Finding my partner's emails had been a message sent to me from my Angels and Spirit Guides so I would never go back with him again! To me this was proof that I was being divinely guided and it lifted some of the heaviness away from my heart. For I knew at that moment I would not be so easily led by the strong male ego again; I would not worry so much about what my partner is thinking and feeling or always put his needs before mine because eventually, as I am putting all my attention on him, I will lose *my-Self* again. I must put attention on *ME*, nurturing myself and the sacred feminine within, because only then can I truly nurture others. It all begins with me loving myself, me feeling good about myself, me being honest with myself and me having peace with myself first. Then I am in the best position to give out *unconditional love* and to have a successful relationship.

In my spiritual books another message repeatedly told through them all is to *love the self*! Self-love does not mean loving ourselves in a vain, egotistical way; it means feeling good and feeling worthy without fear or doubt. Self-love means recognising our divinity within and being open to receive guidance. It means being in alignment and focusing on the things we love which allows us to manifest our dreams, and, most importantly, to truly love one's self means giving love out to others which changes our world and brings love back to us! For if we cannot love who we are right now with all our so-called imperfections, how can others love us?

Like attracts like, therefore if we love and transform ourselves, throwing away our past conditionings, outdated beliefs and useless emotional baggage, and if we strive to be the spiritually best that we can be, we attract that same likeness back. Many people think, *If I find someone to love me then I will be complete*. I do believe in Soul Mates and Twin Flames, but another person does not have to complete me, as this puts an incredible amount of responsibility on someone else for my spiritual growth. This is my own responsibility; it's not up to someone else to make me self-realised and no one can make me truly happy!

We are all yearning to freely express love to each other because love is eternally flowing through our soul and *love is what we are,* and we are all seeking oneness through relationships and sexual union! Yet only when we have *oneness with the love within ourselves can we then have true oneness and union with another* because:

> "When you fall in love with yourself,
> you fall in love with life
> And the whole world falls in love with you!"

The entire experience with my now ex-partner was a very painful, wounding and isolating time for me. Yet it forced me to see that the people who hurt us are the ones we learn from the most! The enlightened ones tell us these people are our biggest teachers, our angels in disguise as they teach us about *self-love and forgiveness*. They test us and give us an opportunity not to react negatively towards them, but to remain calm and to react with love, even after they have caused us to suffer; this is spiritual practice because all unkind behaviour is an unconscious request for peace, love and help!

Through this we learn about ourselves as we are reflections, mirrors and we show each other our fears and negativities that need to be healed because when someone is kind towards us it means we have more kindness to express and when someone is unkind towards us it means we have unkindness in our hearts that needs to be released.

Once someone does something hurtful to us, it is very difficult to forgive them, yet if we can see the reason why it happened and evolve from it then when we do eventually forgive, we become free. For life is a process of letting go and allowing it to be and because the enlightened ones tell us that forgiving someone is one of the biggest ways to give love away to others. Even though I understood this, I did not feel any forgiveness towards my ex-partner as my wounds were too fresh!

The Poet Rumi said,

"The wound is where the light enters"

Every choice I make and every experience I go through are ways for me to remember my truth within, and instead of asking myself, "Why is this happening to me?" or "What have I done to deserve this?" I must ask, "What do I need to learn from this situation?" Once I have understood what I needed to learn it will never repeat itself again! In every lifetime we go through different lessons which enable us to make higher choices about the person we want to be and so create better experiences. In the end *good and bad* are the same; we learn and remember from them all. Maybe I had come to Italy to learn from my life experiences, to find out the truth about my egoic relationship and ultimately remember the truth about myself and the *meaning of love!* At last I am beginning to let go of my resistance and to not feel unworthy any more. At last I am learning to see the beauty and perfection in all things, and at last I am seeing that there is a reason to every relationship and a purpose to every situation!

Eckhart Tolle tells us, from the astounding book *A New Earth:*

> *"Life will give you whatever experience is most helpful for the evolution of your consciousness. How do you know this is the experience you need? Because this is the experience you are having at this moment."*

This is my awakening, my self-realisation and my evolution and I am so lucky to have been woken up now at the age of forty-two as I could have gone on for years being *'spiritually unconscious'*. It has made me stronger and infinitely more compassionate. It's teaching me to love myself, to trust the process of life and to know that my journey to becoming a *self-realised yogini* is the true path for me! I do not hate my ex-partner, (many men have affairs and in Italy they think it's quite normal to do this) for he is the father of my four gorgeous children and, deep down under all the ego and bravado, he is a spiritual man. He just has to find that out without me! I do not want to live with any man at this time in my life…

<blockquote>"I want me!"</blockquote>

Through the challenges, problems and chaos that our relationships and marriages present us with, we awaken to our truth which transforms our negative mind and changes the way we perceive life. This is part of our conscious evolution moving us forever forward and evolving us away from ego personality-based relationships into *Soulful Relationships*. For to truly love does not mean to *take* everything from the other and when they are empty throw them away! No, this is the old egoic way of loving where we connect on a lower level and fall in love with the physical body. In the *'New Soulful way of Loving we give to one another'* we have a higher connection and we love each other's Spirit and the God and Goddess within. Consequently as we grow older we are still in love with that person because we did not fall in love with what they looked like – we fell in love with how they feel and with their spiritual desires – we fell in love with their *Soul!* Thus physical love will never last, but *divine love lasts forever!*

A relationship of the soul means loving without limitations, prejudices, judgements, rules or fear. It uplifts each other by raising the Kundalini energy naturally up the spine where it opens our chakras to bring growth, change and the transformation of both partners and allows us to take love energy freely because *divine love never runs out*! This is a holy relationship which motivates us to be of service to others and moves us into common unity (community) and unconditional love for all beings, not just for one special being. Thus it is the soulful union of finding God, of finding love within and learning to love everyone and everything!

"Love is the New Religion of the Twenty-First Century!"

After finding out the truth about my ex-partner, I knew I needed a check-up and some tests as I was sure he had not used any protection while he was with all those girls and then with me – it made me feel very unclean. I went to see my gynaecologist who is a lovely Italian lady that helped me through Rocco's birth and thought we had a beautiful family. I told her everything that had happened and she was so upset for me and the children. She looked at me with large sad eyes, gave me a heartfelt cuddle and covered my cheeks with Italian kisses. The next time I saw her she reassured me that all the tests had come back negative, but found that I had developed a fibroid in my uterus the size of a small egg! (A fibroid is a small cyst or growth.) Christiane Northrup MD who wrote the enlightening book *Women's Bodies, Women's Wisdom* tells us that, "Fibroids are the result of flowing life-energy, prana into dead ends such as jobs or relationships that we have outgrown," – how true – and in Louise Hay's book *You Can Heal Your Life,* which is like my health bible, she tells us, "Fibroids come from nursing the hurt of a partner, a blow to the feminine ego," and she calls it the "he done me wrong" syndrome!

I was prescribed oral medication to take over the next few months to shrink it down, but it was so disgusting to drink – I took it for a few days then put the rest in the rubbish. I told myself I would make it disappear with my positive yogic lifestyle, my meditations and me loving myself! For the more I accept and love me, the more loving, happy vibes I give off which changes the atmosphere in any place or situation I am in. This is my magnetism and charisma which attracts amazing things and people to me, and even if others are negative it does not affect me because my aura of positivity and love repels all negativity. I know that for me to experience a soulful relationship in the future I must think love, feel love, speak love and be love which opens my heart, and as I give out these emotions I will attract back an *exquisitely spiritual, sensuously stimulating and divinely passionate union with another soul!*

"Love opens our heart. Fear closes our heart!"

The Heart sends out the strongest signals and messages; therefore to manifest anything we must come from the heart, not the egoic mind. To attract a soul mate – and family, friends, business partners, teachers as well as lovers and life partners are all our soul mates that we have been with in other lives – we must quieten our mind and put all our loving feelings into intending, visualising and truly believing that we will meet them. A soul mate activates the channels of energy within our heart, mind and soul so that we have a soul connection which propels us to want to be with them again. If this connection is romantic when we touch each other we feel a jolt or thrill in the heart and sexual organs which are our spiritual/sexual energies embracing! Twin Flames have an even stronger connection. They are one soul in two bodies and may have been separated through many lifetimes to learn lessons and to evolve. When they are born into physicality and eventually meet again, their union helps awaken people to Divine Love which accelerates Heaven on Earth! It is believed at this spiritual time many Twin Flames are incarnating to aid humanity's *Ascension!*

Love is attraction and we attract all the things we love and focus upon as everything in the universe vibrates with the same pranic love/light energy; *thus we must give love to receive love!* Practising yoga and meditation purifies our mind, detoxifies our body and heightens our vibration so that we send out the correct, positive signals to attract a soul mate or twin flame to us. The Heart Chakra is the level where one begins to love oneself and all beings unconditionally, and according to the Ancient Yogis this Lotus of the Heart is the centre where spiritual consciousness is concentrated. Meditating on the *'Star Light of our Soul'* within, we begin to give, receive and be the perfect Divine Love that *God intended us to be!*

To attract more love, peace and compassion into my life I created a Heart Chakra Meditation which everyone can practise. Firstly I sit in a comfortable position on the floor with my spine straight. I close my eyes and breathe yogically for a few minutes, completely relaxing myself with my breath, becoming present in the moment and silencing my mind. Then I bring awareness to my heart chakra in the spine at the level of the sternum and begin meditating on this chakra, visualising its sacred green light and sensing its calming subtle vibration. I feel the rhythm of my beating heart, I feel its love energy becoming stronger and vibrating more intensely, because with every breath I take my Anahata Chakra is spinning faster and opening its twelve lotus flower petals. I begin to sense a warm, loving, blissful energy emanating from this heightened chakra which fills my whole being.

I start to chant its mantra Yam very softly on the out breath as my voice has a healing effect upon it. I begin to resonate with the sacred sound and vibration of my heart and I visualise its green colour all over my chest. I release any fear, pain, grief or negativity that I may have been holding onto in my heart from this life and past lives, and I observe in my mind's third eye the star light of my soul. I then experience my soul consciousness in every cell of my body and feel it radiating with bliss! I become *'One with Spirit and One with Love'* and vibrate this healing energy out, giving love to all sentient beings on Earth and to any Soul Mate or Twin Flame that I wish to attract. I stay with this beautiful feeling for as long as I want and feel compassion for myself and others. I thank the Universe, God and I surrender and allow transcendent love to guide my life. I breathe yogically again, opening my eyes and integrating that peaceful, loving feeling into every thought, word and action throughout my day which increases love in the world and attracts peace and love back to me!

It's hard for us to feel the energy of our soul because it's clouded over by fear, negativity, ignorance and the ego. However with spiritual discipline we can remove this covering and the truth shines forth, liberating us from previous karma and transforming our minds into pure love consciousness.

When others see my struggles and look at some of the awakenings I had to go through on my spiritual journey to find my-self, and eventually someday have enlightenment, they may say to themselves; "Oh no, looking for the truth of Self, of God, of Love within is far too difficult, I don't think I will bother just now, maybe later!" It may look to be the hardest path, but it is the only path to infinite wisdom and freedom from fear, doubt and delusion. We may travel to other countries seeking different religions and praying to many Gods, searching for what we all want, which is love and happiness, only to find that coming home it was always within our reach – it was always here inside our heart all along!

For me the true meaning of love is to love myself, love my children, love my family, love my friends, love all beings and love all people deep down for who they are because only by loving all people can we save the world!

"The purpose of human love is to awaken love for God, Love is the Divine Power that shines through us All!"

CHAPTER 9

THE LAWS OF KARMA, ATTRACTION AND LOVE

There is nothing on Earth you cannot be, do or have and your work here is to seek joy! As you think thoughts that feel good to you, you will be in harmony with who you really are. Seek joy first and all the growth that you could ever imagine will joyously and abundantly come to you.

ABRAHAM-HICKS

During the following months I enjoyed being single and started embracing my womanhood. When I meditated I had sublime sensations of love filling my heart and I felt a deeper sense of sacred empowerment and connection to Spirit. I realised that finding out the truth about my relationship was something I needed to go through to finally end it. The whole ordeal was inviting me to consciously evolve and my emotional wounds were moving me forward to follow the spiritual calling of my soul. I was determined not to hold on to any negative feelings inside my energetic pain-body, but through yoga and Kriya meditations I would release them and therefore not be affected by them in the future. I also accepted that I had *self-created* all these situations and experiences here in Italy so I could move through my blocks and limitations and be *who I truly am*. I saw that through fear and my negative, deluded mind I had created a failed yoga retreat and egoic/larmic relationship. But now I knew for sure that through love, through God through my positive truthful heart, I could begin again, and I could use the laws of karma, attraction and love to create a successful yoga retreat and eventually a soulful relationship!

My close family and friends were a fantastic support to me through the break-up with my ex-partner. My parents helped me with the children and babysat when I taught a yoga class or had a coffee in town, and my girlfriends in England called me up making sure I was OK. I felt truly blessed to have such a caring family and friends and began to understand its true meaning. I saw that the family unit needs to be an environment where unconditional love, kindness and compassion are given to all its members and that it must be a place of warmth, safety and acceptance for women and men to nurture their children so they can bring up compassionate human beings. As our society awakens we are realising that the pain and heartache some people have suffered in family life can be transcended and thus not passed on to the next generation. As love prevails we can learn to overcome self-blame and unworthiness to form devoted empathetic relationships and families which support all children and nurture all people. Through the example of family caring we can bring love awareness into every school and institution so the next generations develop spiritual values which will reduce the destructive, materialistic world view that is still so prevalent today.

I see how wise it is to have an extended family, as resources are put together for the good of all, children are taught knowledge and kindness by all members and learn to respect the older generations. Young people today are living alone and having children, yet what can they teach them about love and truth when they themselves are still learning what it means to be an honourable person. Looking after and educating our young is the most important job of all and needs to be shared by the elders in every family and community so they can pass on their life experience and help solve problems with their wisdom. Here in Italy most people appreciate the benefit of the extended family; they live together and take care of their elderly who contribute with funds and become involved in bringing up the little ones.

I have not made any close Italian friends while living in Italy, but my English girlfriend has become very dear to me and the only person here that I can talk to on a spiritual level. All my other girlfriends live in England and France; we have known each other for over twenty-five years and they are my *'soul sisters'*. When we were younger, we had many fantastic experiences together and have always been there for one another through all the good and bad times. When I lived in England we would meet up in London where we'd drink champagne and go out dancing – causing a sensation wherever we went.

My girlfriends are extremely beautiful, vivacious and the most charming, compassionate women. I feel there is a divine connection between us and I missed them all so much!

During the enchanting springtime, two of my girlfriends called and said they were flying over to stay with me for a few days because I needed to have some fun! It was exciting picking them up at the airport as we had not seen each other for a couple of years and we chatted non-stop all the way home. They could not believe how much my three daughters had grown and they hadn't even seen my son and both commented on how handsome he was. Since the weather was warm, in the daytime we booked sunbeds at the exclusive beach bars and relaxed in the glorious sun, and in the early evenings we put on our party dresses and high heels and had luxurious dinners along the stylish Riviera delle Palme while gazing at the incredible sea view. My generous girlfriends paid for me and I vowed next time I would treat them.

On their last night we went out dancing, letting ourselves dance free and becoming wild women again. It was fun catching the eye of other men looking at me and, although I did not want to be with any of them, it made me feel good and confident that I was still desirable! At the end of the night we drank herbal tea, talked, laughed and I read their Tarot cards which were unbelievably precise. Waving goodbye to them at the airport I had tears in my eyes and wondered when I would see them again!

Having a close family and great friends is a wonderful environment for spiritual growth and realisation. None of us are perfect and we all have the false ego, yet if we can recognise its wrong behaviour and look at each other with love and forgiveness – trying to be honest with each other, having trust in each other and admitting that we are wrong sometimes – we can all evolve together. Every family goes through problems and all people have made mistakes in life which have been self-created for our higher good and chosen by us to give us a chance to heal. I am trying to react with love towards my family and friends and to communicate with them and with all beings in truth and compassion, giving the most important gift which I can give – *my true honest self*. I want to have the courage to be who I am in every moment and in every situation because in our innermost truth we can do no wrong.

"For we are here to educate and learn from each other,
To love and forgive each other and to set each other free"

I am learning not to allow my lower nature to judge or criticise my family, friends or others, but to respect their different points of view and to accept them just the way they are. I need to see that when others express negativity, resentment or anger these emotions are the unconscious reactions of their pain-body and it's not their fault. They cannot help it as it's just part of their past conditioning, incorrect thinking and fear, and they are out of alignment with their true selves and identifying with ego. I understand I cannot change them; in fact I cannot change anyone. The only person I can change is me! Then leading by example maybe others will follow my truth because:

"Truth is Infectious!"

The Ancient Yogis tell us we are all *conditioned souls* as the values, beliefs and social conditionings that we grow up with from our parents, grandparents, schools, religions, the government and even past lives contribute to the forming of our egos, how we perceive ourselves and ultimately the person we become. We unconsciously take on these mental states, thinking thoughts and performing habits which are related to them, and when we are going through challenging situations we may react with fear from our recalled past conditionings. Some of my family's beliefs and conditionings are: 'the world is getting worse; money is scarce; thinking negatively; we are all separate; not being able to show love easily and we will all get sick and grow old early'. These conditionings are nobody's fault, but have been passed down collectively from generation to generation. This is Ancestral Karma which causes personal patterns that make us create the same things over again or to live identical lives to our parents and family.

Once I realise that my parents' beliefs and the way they were brought up was just outdated egoic and social conditioning passed down from their parents, grandparents, teachers and the environment, I can begin to comprehend them better. When I sit down and really talk with my parents about their childhood and their parents' lives, I understand their behaviour more and have true compassion and forgiveness towards them. If we can accept that our parents did the best they could with the knowledge and awareness they had, and that once we let go of the hurt, anger and wrongdoings we think they caused us (for attachment to these negative feelings only makes us feel bad) then love flows freely from us to them without us saying or doing anything!

I could see that most of us, including my friends, family and me, live in the past and future. For our reactions are automatic, either coming from our past experiences or from our future wanting where we are always waiting for our lives to begin; waiting for that holiday to give us joy, waiting until we finish that course to be happy, waiting until we win the lottery to be content or waiting for our house to be sold so we can be free. But this is our life *now!* This powerful moment of now is where everything happens, where the past is forgiven and the future is our next feeling, thought and experience we are choosing in this very instant. The miracle is always in this present moment because the present moment always gives us truth and freedom. I have to forget my past and the past of others, renewing myself in the positive now and meeting others only in the loving present, not the judgemental past.

I see how important it is not to constantly seek approval from my parents, teachers and loved ones. I must think for myself, not from the past conditioning of others or from my family's ancestral karma. I must forget the pre-conceived ideas and mistaken perceptions of other people's self-seeking egos and make up my own mind about things. I must unlearn the wrong, segregating teaching passed down from our misguided society and trust in my unique being to think newer, higher, kinder thoughts which helps integrate, elevate and heal every other mind.

> "When we change our mind about the world,
> Seeing it with clear vision as it truly is, in its magical,
> majestic, safe and benevolent state,
> It will become this!"

At that time I only had a couple of ladies coming to my yoga classes and money was extremely tight for us. Every month my ex-partner in London sent money over, yet relying on someone whose life was so chaotic was stressful and worrying. His jobs were unreliable, not paying that well and with our enormous bills the money was not enough to look after us. I went to the Italian social security office to see if I could get some child benefits or family tax credits for my four children as I received none from Italy or England which I thought was wrong as I believe the welfare of children is important. But the very helpful man said there was no money that I was entitled to and the only solution for me was to get a job! Yes, OK, but who would look after my children? They went to school half days, my mum was not well enough to look after them on her own for very long periods and to cook their lunch or dinners, and my dad worked irregular hours.

I explained the situation to my ex-partner, but he just shouted at me down the phone to "Go get a normal job!" Yoga he said was my hobby and not a job. Well, with four young children to care for, being English and in this sleepy region of Italy where he had not been able to find work, it wasn't going to be easy. My Italian was not good enough to work in the shops or supermarkets; I tried the only disco in the area to work on the coat check, and although I still looked great for my age, when they saw how old I was on my Italian I.D. I never heard from them again! The Mayor's secretary helped me to get a cleaning job five mornings a week, and it was the hardest work I had ever done in my life!

This lovely lady had me doing all of her dirtiest jobs and wanted every single surface in her very modern house steam-cleaned with a steam machine that I had to carry around with me which weighed a ton. She lived in a town by the beach which was twenty minutes away from me by car, using up five euros of petrol a day. I worked fifteen hours a week and when the tax and petrol was taken off I ended up with forty euros in my pocket. When I left the house in the early mornings my youngest child Rocco would cry for me; it was horrible and every time I finished work I would end up crying in my car! I just couldn't do it any more.

I even got my courage together and tried working as a hostess in an Italian 'nightclub' which was awful! All those poor girls, lots of them mothers who had no one and no government to support them. Sitting around, drinking champagne and chatting up dishonest, lonely men from 11pm to 5am in the morning – it eerily reminded me of my escorting days but with much less pay! I stuck it out for four nights and was probably one of the oldest girls there. It was extremely demoralising and I got an awful throat infection from the oppressive, smoke-filled disco interior; yet at least with the money I made I was able to pay off some bills!

I tried not to be negative and thought if I focused on the things that made me feel good and gave out positive vibrations, something better would come along! I buried myself in my spiritual books and ancient yogic texts once again and was amazed how they tell us in different ways about the same Eternal Truths, Secrets to Life and Divine Universal Laws. These truths, secrets and laws maintain the life and evolution of creation! When we live by them our mind, body and soul comes into alignment and we vibrate love energy out which elevates the entire atmosphere and helps us to manifest our dreams. These are the ones that mean the most to me:

A Divine Law, "We Create our own Reality". Everything is spiritual; the universe is creation, from the Divine Heart and Mind of God which we are connected to. We are a co-creator with the Source of all Creation and we create our bodies, our life experiences and material things by what we think, feel and intend.

A Secret to Life, "Giving is Receiving". Giving selflessly automatically causes its opposite reaction of receiving. When we give love, let go of fear and are grateful for our blessings and life lessons, we make space to receive abundance.

The Eternal Truth of Forgiveness! Forgive yourself, forgive everyone else and react with forgiveness because this sets you free! When we forgive, this energy goes out and the universe brings it back to us as joy!

The Secret to Peace is this Divine Moment! Only this moment exists! All power and peace comes from being in the new thought of now, where the past cannot hurt us, where the future has no hold over us, but where we are all 'forgiven' and can begin again.

An Eternal Truth, "We Are All One". Everything has Spirit, we are an eternal part of the Collective Soul Consciousness of every living being and all things are connected by love energy in our world and universe.

The Eternal Truth and Divine Law of Love! There is only Love! God is divine love and love is our ultimate truth and our most sublime feeling. The law of love attracts all the people, places, things and situations to us, therefore let us all choose love over fear because the more love we feel and give, the more love we receive.

One law which has had a great effect on me is the *Natural Law of Cause and Effect, Karma.* When I was younger I was caught up in a world of materialism. I had lots of money and expensive, designer clothes which fed my ego and made me want to keep on taking and needing more money and more things. Yet these past years in Italy I haven't had much money or possessions which have helped me to understand how the law of karma works as I am learning to be a *giver, not a taker!*

A couple of weeks after my disastrous attempts to get a job, I began waking up earlier. After performing Surya Yoga and Kriya meditations in the warm early sun, I would pray, thank and ask God to please *give* every soul on earth: *peace and love, compassion and forgiveness and prosperity and perfect health.* I did it every morning with complete sincerity and I knew it was having a profound effect on me because, as I walked through town or on the land in nature, I felt I was naturally learning to give of myself. To give out positive thoughts, feelings, words and actions to the people, animals, trees and plants around me. To *give out love* and to treat others with respect, talking about them in a good way and pointing out their talents and positive qualities.

As Jesus said;

"Do unto others as you would have it done unto you."

The ancient Upanishads tell us that karma is the instrument of God which keeps the cycle of reincarnation continuing for each individual life on earth. Karma in Sanskrit means action. It is the result and consequence of every thought, feeling, word and action we made previously and the natural outcome of all our positive or negative choices and desires we experienced before. Therefore my thoughts are forming my future and my destiny is in my own hands and once I behave in a more conscious way I become the cause of my experiences, not at the mercy of them. I am now trying to make every action a sacred loving action as to me the law of karma is also the *Law of Love!*

For the more peacefully aware, compassionate and loving I become, by the *Grace of God, by 'Divine Forgiveness'* I will break free from the chain of karma and my actions will no longer create any reactions! My Sat Guru tells us karma is stored in our DNA inside the nitrogen nubs along the spine, and as we practise Kundalini Kriya Yoga this breathing up and down the spine rubs off the karma.

Maharishi Mahesh Yogi wrote in his fascinating book *Science of Being and Art of Living:*

> *"The expression of goodness, sweetness or love to a child produces a loving and life-supporting influence through the whole cosmos. One harsh, cruel word to a person will produce that influence of harshness and cruelty throughout creation. The reaction created by these vibrations as they influence the Universe travels back to the individual as Karma"*

The other powerful law that has affected me is the *Natural Law of Attraction* which I find absolutely incredible because again, the law of attraction is also the *Law of Love!* Love energy holds everything together in creation. It brings harmony to the universe, pulls everything to me and when I let go of trying to be in control or thinking about past or future, I become aligned with the giving and receiving of love. I am beginning to understand how the law of attraction works and how I have been guided by Spirit and given the little things that I have loved, thought and meditated upon.

I had been using an Italian computer to write this book for quite a number of years, but it was complicated to use because my Italian was so limited. What I really needed was an 'English laptop', yet where on earth was I going to find one in Italy, without any money. All I wanted to do was to write! I imagined myself writing on a new computer and I told all my friends and family that I had to have an English laptop. I must have been giving out a *strong vibrational feeling and powerful heartfelt desire* for it because my old college friend called me up saying a colleague in his London office had a laptop that he never used and I could have it!

I was amazed and realised these natural laws were working for me because when I put my awareness on something with a lot of feeling and faith it makes the attraction *happen faster*. It's working all around me every day in little ways; I just have to be thankful and open to receive it.

Everything on Earth, all the buildings, computers and aeroplanes, everything first began as thoughts and images inside people's minds. They put *their awareness, their love* on their heart's desires and *intended* and *asked* for them, then received inspiration to take action and manifest them into their lives. To attract our material and spiritual goals we must be present, give thanks and believe that they will come to us. We must focus on them with love; for love is the magnetic force which heightens our magnetism and brings mind, body and soul into vibrational alignment allowing us to co-create with the awesome power of the Universe, God. The creation process is always *"Ask for it, Visualise it, Feel the Love of having it and be Open to Receive it!"*

Our thoughts, emotions and consciousness are energy travelling at a higher, faster rate of vibration. Energy is atoms and atoms are made up of love; they respond with more of the same love energy which goes out along the universal energy field to influence external events and attract all the people, things and situations into our lives. Therefore we must be conscious about the energy we are giving out and always think of the outcome, putting our attention on the same thoughts, desiring and choosing the same thing, and not changing our minds all the time. Also we must be careful that we are not being consumed by the self-centred egoic mind and asking for negative things which may hurt others – but we have self-control and ask for things that spiritually evolve us and humanity.

Albert Einstein said:

"Everything is energy and that's all there is to it.
Match the frequency of the reality you want and you cannot help but get that reality.
It can be no other way. This is not philosophy.
This is physics!"

This is the most astounding secret that everyone in this world has the right to know. *"When we form a thought or desire in our creative, present minds, then visualise on the outcome with love and feel that we already have it with faith, and be open enough with gratitude to receive. Divine Intelligence will give us messages, coincidences and inspirations to attract all things to us. Every thought which is meditated upon, every loving desire that is felt and every word which has thankfulness behind it will be expressed as action and manifested into our lives!"*

God has given humanity the most wonderful magical gift; to use and control our minds so we can be, do or have anything we love! For *miracles and magic* are simply a change in consciousness, a change in perception and a change of heart! This is more powerful than poverty, any terrible situation and all our fears and doubts. All we have to do is raise our vibration by searching for loving thoughts, caring about the way we feel and being present in the moment because Spirit only works in present time will we then be in control of our lives because we hold the key and power over all our situations and circumstances!

I knew then I had to use the law of attraction and love to bring more money to me and my family as we were struggling to pay our enormous electricity bills. We had sold all our jewellery a while ago and I needed to come up with something else to help us out. I also knew I had to change my negative thoughts about money as the previous thoughts I had constantly been thinking had turned into negative beliefs. Brain studies now reveal that thoughts produce the same mental instructions as actions and that visualising affects our brain in a similar way as doing the real thing. Scientists have proven that the repetition of images, thoughts and visualisations start to fire the neuron connections inside the brain in the same sequence, over and over which ingrain into the subconscious mind where they become a belief or habit, and that by changing our thoughts the brain develops new neuron connections and grows new brain cells to become rewired and thus create new beliefs.

The negative, limiting belief which I carried around with me for a long time was *'money is the root of all evil'*. I said it to everyone and I totally believed it; however this was wrong because money is bits of paper and metal used for exchange – it's not evil. Only now do I see that working as a topless dancer and high-class escort when I was younger were not the best of ways to earn a living and I believe this made me view money as negative, fearful and evil. Lack of money was also part of my social conditioning that I had grown up with which had been passed down from one working-class generation to the next and part of my ancestral karma that I had accumulated.

Consequently this incorrect thinking has made it increasingly difficult for me to attract prosperity into my life. I realised I had to stop putting attention on my lack of money or on what I don't have, and change my focus by putting my attention on being thankful for what I do have and feeling good about money; also I must not criticise people who are wealthy because the Universe, God is always attracting back to me what I am focusing on. I need to connect to my true self and be in soul alignment where I feel good and abundant, where I say yes to prosperity and help as many people around me as possible to receive and benefit from abundance and prosperity, as the more I help and give to others the more I help and give to myself.

This *'Giving is Receiving'* is a secret to life which the big wealthy corporations and banks understand; for they hoard money and resources, systematically keeping masses of people in poverty which breeds money-related crimes, violence and more inequality in our world. I believe as humanity's consciousness evolves we will use the law of attraction and love to find new spiritual ways of being and giving, and in our children's future money will be obsolete.

Subsequently I began to positively pray, meditate and ask Spirit for help. I focused on the good things in my life and I lovingly intended, visualised and believed that money would come to us. Coincidentally and miraculously, a message and idea was given to me! One morning while I was sitting having my favourite macchiato coffee in the local bar in town, I had a chance meeting with a friend. He told me that I could make a lot of money by selling off some of our fifteen olive trees! I then remembered that the lovely Italian man we had bought all our palm trees and tropical plants from, had an enormous plant nursery down by the beach. He knew about our situation and would often come up to see how the English family were doing and always gave us free fruit trees and plants. I called him up and in my terrible Italian told him how we needed money and asked if he would be interested in buying some olive trees for his nursery.

The very next day this marvellous man drove over to our house and walked around the land tying red ribbons around the trees that he wanted to buy. He said he would send the diggers over to remove the trees in the next few weeks, and then proceeded to place a large sum of money into my hand! I was so thankful to this man, so thankful to Spirit and so thankful to the law of attraction and love, and immediately drove to the post office to pay the electricity bill so we wouldn't be cut off. During the following weeks we waited for our Italian friend to send the diggers over, but this amazingly generous man never did take any of his olive trees!

Afterwards I felt myself breaking free from my negative beliefs about money and acknowledged that I was creating new neuron connections so I no longer impulsively reacted in the same old conditioned way. I was reprogramming my thoughts, beliefs and conditionings which I had become attached to and which had turned into deep-seated habits because my habits are not fixed; everything in my mind and body is changeable!

I create my own reality and I do this by the way I feel because we live in a vibrational universe which mirrors the emotional vibrations we give out! Therefore I must be careful to choose the things I love and turn away from the things I do not want; otherwise even the unwanted things shall be attracted to me and show up in my life. Most of us are unconsciously creating the same reality over and over again, yet when we understand there are an infinite number of creatable realities and possibilities to choose from, we can consciously choose the highest possibility which gives us the highest experience.

Negative attraction is what happens when we allow the ego's uncontrolled thoughts to run around free in our minds; however through meditation we control our minds, and put our attention on the things we love. As we begin to use our creative imagination to think, feel and visualise the same things over and over, again and again, this energy will *attract more of the same like energy that sticks together forming layers, one on top of the other, which eventually creates physical matter!*

My Sat Guru tells us when lots of like-minded people get together projecting the same peace and love thoughts, feelings, desires and words out into the world, they have an extraordinary power and, through their collective consciousness, they change physical reality and produce the desired effects and results they want. He calls such a gathering of souls "*Come Unity Humanity*" (Community Humanity). Changing my thoughts, feelings and vibrations is what the laws of karma, attraction and love are all about and it's how I create magic and miracles in my life! To change them I must be aware of how I feel! If I feel positive, I am giving out positive energy vibrations and will attract something good to me, but if I feel negative, I am giving out negative energy vibrations and will attract something bad to me. I need to feel the wisdom of my heart and soul which is the truth of God within because my:

"Feelings are the language of my soul!"

When I am truly grateful and give thanks to God I make space to receive abundance and, if it's in accordance with my soul's purpose and with the *New World Vision of Peace, Love, Unity and Equality, all will be given to me!* For Divine Intelligence always reflects and mirrors my inner world with my outer world – as within so without, as above so below! This is the natural magical law of karma, attraction and love; imagine how fantastic the world will be when we all live by these divine laws, truths and secrets to life!

We shall join together using our minds and feelings responsibly and collectively to create a new society where all people will be individually happier with no more hunger, no more poverty, no more inequality, no more loneliness, no more competition and no more separation. There will be enough energy, food and abundance for all with no more aggression, conflict or wars. All people will live and evolve together in spiritual harmony with everyone realising that we are all connected by the same sacred love energy that lies within every human, animal, insect, tree, plant and stone. For we are a co-creator with God, this ancient wisdom is our sacred power and our inner mystical attraction, and it is miraculous. We are living in a magnificent universe full of infinite possibilities!

Laurie Cabot said in her enlightening book *The Power of the Witch* that I read when I was eighteen:

"We are not isolated individuals leading isolated lives. We are literally plugged into the entire Universe, what happens on the other side of the Earth affects us, our actions have cosmic repercussions. It is as humbling as it is awe-inspiring to realise the influence we possess and the incredible responsibility to use our powers wisely and for the good of all!"

As I slowly become an *awakened soul* I see that if I feel the love of teaching people on my yoga retreat; if I feel the joy of helping others find their own spirituality; if I feel my heart's desire of sitting in my garden by my Lotus flower pond and if I am open with positivity to receive, I will manifest my dream into my reality.

Albert Einstein said;

"Imagination is more important than Knowledge!

Each one of us is on a spiritual journey. We are all experiencing and remembering and we can have all the things we love for ourselves and for the good of humanity. Therefore let us follow our bliss and begin *dreaming* our life into being and let us have faith in the invisible magic power of the Divine that shines through us all!

"You are a Spiritual Being!
Believe that you are limitless then begin dreaming,
loving and meditating
Upon the amazing person that you are,
So you can 'BE' this person now and
Attract your Divine Life!"

CHAPTER 10

OUR CHILDREN ARE OUR HEROES

When we teach our children to think and feel good in every moment. To know they are always divinely protected and guided. To understand they can be, do or have anything they want in life so long as it's for the good of all. To learn to love themselves and all others, realising Humanity is ONE! When we teach our children about their Divine Love Energy within and as they give it out to the rest of the world. Only then shall we have Peace on Earth.

JOANNE LEE PHILPOT

My children really are my *'heroes and my heroines'*; all through these difficult times in Italy they are the ones who have looked after me. I truly believe that going through challenging experiences has made them view life in a much more realistic way, helping them to understand that things can go wrong and to see the positive in every negative situation. My children make me laugh with joy at all the funny, innocent things they say and do, and they are teaching me to let go and be my spontaneous true self a lot more. Living close to my parents and having land to run around on has been a great advantage for them as they have developed a deep respect for the older generation and the natural world. It's delightful for us to play with our younger generation, feeling like a child again, having fun, and remaining youthful and carefree – for children are our *teachers, our medicine and our meditation!*

I thank God for my children and tell them I love them all the time! I tell them they are beautiful on the outside, but more importantly that they are beautiful on the inside, in their kind, compassionate, giving hearts which teaches them to appreciate, respect and love their true magnificent selves. For there is nothing sweeter in this world than the love of a mother for her child as every mother is a representation of the *Divine Universal Mother of All* and we should thank ourselves for doing such a remarkable job of bringing up the next generation. We must see that when women and children are cared for, protected and nurtured in society, this nurtures the future generations of our species and every other species on the planet. My spiritual children, all spiritual children of the world and the next generation of spiritual children to come will be living and creating much more from their Spirit Soul and energy bodies. They will be born with more awareness of the light within; some will already be born *'awakened beings'* and all will help transform Humanity into Divinity.

> "We must make it our mission to ensure every child grows up happy, this will bring harmony and serenity and peace back to our world."

I am helping my children to believe in themselves and, most importantly, to think for themselves and to question everything! For each one has their own issues to work through and their own purpose to fulfil in this lifetime. This is why I am making them understand the divine laws of karma, attraction and love so they can feel and visualise wonderful things and therefore have wonderful things. I feed my children a wholesome yogic Sattvic diet which is low in sugar and fats and high in vitamins, nutrients and pranic energy, as a bad diet can cause negative thinking, aggressive behaviour, childhood illnesses and obesity which produces self-esteem and health problems as they grow. I teach them fun yoga and create guided meditations for them, which support their creative imaginations.

Every full moon my children and I practise our peace and love meditation and ritual outside, surrounded in wondrous nature with all our candles and incense. We chant mantras, play drums and dance around the fire; we make our wishes to the moon, heal the Earth and give out peace and love to all the people in the world – especially to the bad ones! I feel it is important for children and all of us to have rituals and ceremonies, as they help us experience the *sacredness of life and connect us to the earth and to each other!*

When the hot summer months came around again, our sleepy region of Italy started to wake up! I took my children to the rides, trampolines and big swimming pool with its fantastic water slide, and to our favourite secluded beach where we collected shells to paint, swam in the warm sea and lay under the sun that turned our bodies golden brown and our hair blonde. The friendly locals called us the Barbie 'famiglia' (family) and asked in astonishment if all the children were mine as these days, because the cost of living is so expensive in Italy, most women were only having one child per family which is not very good for the Italian economy, yet extremely good for the world's over-population problem. On balmy nights my children played outside on the land with all of nature to keep them company; they climbed the olive trees, played on the homemade swings and had fun in the plastic swimming pool until late.

When it was stormy or raining they used their creative imagination to make up games inside the house and they have all developed an amazing skill of arts, crafts, music, dancing and singing. We haven't got a television, only a computer that I download cartoons, movies, documentaries and art programmes on. I am careful what I expose my children to as most of the boys' animations on TV are about fighting and killing with negative, violent images that affect their minds, and the girls' animations are about what you look like, shopping, make-up and clothes. It will be amazing when we create children's TV in a spiritually conscious way! It could be about saving people around the world from natural disasters and helping them build homes, grow food and create their own energy in advanced futuristic ways; or fighting to save children in third world countries from hunger by sharing resources and flying in food and medicine in fantastically fast super-jets and high-tech ships; or travelling out in space and meeting highly evolved beings who wish to share their technology and help humanity. This is exciting in a positive way!

Towards the end of summer my two eldest daughters both entered a competition called Cantaragazzi (singing children) which was held one magical night on a stage outside the strikingly-lit town hall in Ripatransone. There were about two hundred people watching and five judges from outside of town. Through the previous summer months my two daughters and twenty young girls and boys chose their songs and rehearsed every week with their music teacher from school. When the night of the competition arrived, I dressed Lola and Gina up and put a little make-up on them both. My parents and some of our friends had come to cheer them on and when they each sang their songs we all had tears in our eyes. I felt so proud of my daughters! I couldn't believe how beautiful they were and how moved I was by their amazing voices and, although young, they were confident and at ease on stage, smiling as they sang.

Once they called out Lola's name as the winner we all erupted into a screaming, clapping frenzy! It was quite unbelievable; she won an enormous cup and even Gina, who was the youngest child to enter the competition, won a Barbie doll to her delight. They had their pictures taken on stage with the Mayor of Ripatransone for the local newspaper and on the drive home that evening my dad kept sounding the horn of the car waking up the entire neighbourhood because we were all so happy. I felt our *Angels* had helped in giving us a fantastic night and it seemed to make the problems of the past few years fade into insignificance.

I believe it's important for children to release their negative toxic energy by running around and singing and dancing their hearts out which brings them into the present moment and makes them feel *alive and one with life*. At least once a week I put my favourite music on and we dance together around the house. Dancing, singing and making music are *'energy tools'* that create positive energy within and help us feel joyful. When I was younger I loved *dancing with joy*, as this was my way of expressing myself. I was the life and soul of every party and would always get everyone up dancing. When I dance I let myself go, and I have complete freedom in the moment, releasing any worries and losing my ego to be in soul alignment.

In England I used to go to yoga dance meditation evenings which I will have on my retreat. Yoga dance meditation includes yoga postures and different slow and fast rhythms of music with each rhythm meaning a different stage of spiritual awakening. It allows us to let go and express from our hearts which transforms our minds and awakens us to feel the ecstasy of love energy flowing through our body! The last rhythm of music slows us down and takes us deep within, leading to blissful meditation and a feeling of oneness with the source of creation.

Music, singing, dance, festivals and rituals join us together, giving us unity and meaning. Most indigenous tribes around the world dance to release themselves and to become closer to Spirit. Indigenous music arouses love which fuels empathy towards one another and interweaves with the planetary heartbeat and vibration of Mother Earth! For the whole universe is moving, vibrating and dancing with joy! It's just that we women and men are still holding on to our egos which are caused by our past conditionings, karma and separation from love. Dancing helps us to break free of the ego; it is an expression of our *joyful divine self*, and when we sing or dance in the name of the divine, our karma dissipates, our ego dissolves and we become one with all things.

William W. Purkey tells us:

"You've gotta dance like there's nobody watching, love like you've never been hurt, sing like there's nobody listening. And live like it's Heaven on Earth"

In our local school the teachers are brilliant and each teacher educates the same class of children for the first five years which creates a very strong bond with each individual child. I thought the older children received far too much homework which did not leave them much time to be a playful, happy child and that the school only seemed interested in teaching mathematics and Italian. The teaching was extremely academic and boring as there was not much *creativity or freedom of expression* and hardly any art, crafts or music being taught and no drama, dance or cooking classes. To me the school seemed to be overly competitive; everything was about being the best and about winning, yet not much was taught about fairness or caring and sharing for the good of all. I thought my children were being taught an outdated curriculum that was probably the same in other schools all around the world and it was not stimulating them to want to learn or *exciting their passion or feeding their Spirit!*

The world we live in is extremely diverse and we need a diversity of talents to make the world work. Not every child has the same interests or abilities and not all children are academic. Some may be intellectually and logically minded, while others are more into their bodies, needing to release and express their energy through music, singing, drama or dance and others still may feel the creativity of their soul through art, crafts, design or science and technology. As humanity's consciousness evolves, the education system needs a massive overhaul and needs to evolve too. Education must help our children discover their gifts and inner purpose. It has to nurture their talents and connect them to higher projects that need their skills so they can work in jobs that are self-rewarding, valuable and assist in creating a positive future for all. We have to personalise education to meet individual needs and begin teaching our children *holistically* which is mentally, physically, emotionally and spiritually. For they need to study the world as a living organism, to see it as a whole system which is connected and changing and evolving for the better.

Our children's moral outlook is conditioned by the way they have been brought up – from the examples that parents, schools, religions and governments set. Therefore it's important for them to be brought up in loving, caring environments which help them believe in their abilities and in the importance of family so they too can become loving parents. They must be taught from a young age to be knowledgeable and compassionate so they can see the needs and rights of others and have a sense of self-discipline towards themselves and a responsibility towards every living being.

As humanity merges into a New Love Awareness, I believe we will create new free schools teaching *conscious life studies*. Children would learn spiritual values and important ethical social skills to be kind, honest and caring, and they would nurture their creativity and follow their individual passions so they contribute to the world in positive ways.

In these schools, children would be taught divine laws, secrets to life and eternal truths. They would be encouraged to develop emphatic relationships with people and to respect and learn from the older, wiser generations. To learn about different religions and spiritual awareness – therefore having concern towards all peoples and cultures, and towards all animals, trees, and plants, thus caring for nature and all ecosystems. To understand that *giving is receiving* and not hoard money, resources, wealth or food, but care, share and give all beings the *right to a decent life*. To learn to be honest, forgiving and *grateful* for what they receive and *thankful* towards their parents, elders and Spirit which makes space for them to receive abundance.

We would teach our children the power of thoughts and feelings, how they influence external events, and to *focus on the things they love* with faith which benefits them and humanity. To learn to feel good and create themselves in the way they have always dreamed, then using their abilities to give more peace, love, unity and equality to all. To teach them how to grow their own food, build sustainable houses and energy and conserve Mother Earth's resources. To learn to cook, do housework, and be made to do community service and volunteer work to help the elderly, young and those in need. To be encouraged to go outside into nature a lot more and commune with natural beings, feeling the *Sacredness of Life!*

We would help our children know that *there is only love* in this world and everyone has the choice to express the good or evil that resides within their own hearts and minds, we would teach yoga and meditation in all schools so all children may have self-peace and self-love and realise the truth of their eternal soul and that *humanity is one!* Can you imagine what a *wonderful world* we would be living in if these truths were taught in schools and families all around the world! It will take a few generations for the philosophy of spiritual loving values to filter through our children to the mass of humanity and change the negative, selfish world view – but this is already happening!

The Dalai Lama tells us:

"If every eight-year-old in the world is taught meditation,
We will eliminate violence from the world within
One Generation"

My children are my world and at this time, caring for them on my own is a twenty-four hour job; however I do not mind for I know that my personal life will come later on when I am more settled and they are older. My children are my cheeky little angels and I love them all the same. My eldest daughter LOLA has long, cascading hair to her waist and a perfectly angelic face. She is artistic, creative and compassionate, loving all animals and nature and sings amazingly which gives her joy. She is an *old evolved soul* and loves Tarot and Wicca and makes self-esteem posters to encourage other students in school because she wants to change the world! My second daughter GINA is the dazzling beauty queen with luscious curly blonde hair and her papa's big brown eyes. Gina gives me the most amazing massages by walking on my back with her feet, and is extremely supple as she gets into all the yogic asanas! She is a *free spirit* and so sweet and kind and has an incredible voice, singing soulful songs all day long which is her passion! Gina loves make-up so much she put nail varnish on her eyelids by mistake at age three!

My third daughter SIENNA is the prettiest, most adorable little girl who is constantly creating things out of paper and lets snails slime over her hands! She is very friendly, wanting to heal and care for others and likes yoga, the chakras and growing vegetables. However sometimes she fights with her brother who causes her to get hurt and start a crying, screaming tantrum that lasts for an hour – until she eventually calms down with lots of kisses and cuddles. My son ROCCO is a handsome, kind-hearted prince who has the most intense eyes, cute blonde hair and touches your heart when he dazzles you with his incredible smile. He gives you the best kisses and strongest cuddles because he is so affectionate, and is fascinated with action heroes which he loves to draw and wants to have big muscles when he is older. Rocco is another *free spirit* who loves to be nude all the time and has taken his father's place sleeping beside me in my bed every night. Mostly he is a good, kind boy but sometimes he can be very, very naughty!

While I was painting the downstairs hallway with a big pot of white paint, as it was covered in children's hand-prints, something happened and the pot of paint was left on its own for a few minutes. When I came back there was Rocco standing in the paint pot with his clothes and shoes on, covered in white paint up to his chin! He had decided to help us out with the painting by spraying the walls and floor with the roller. It was like a comedy sketch – there was so much paint on the floor as I tried to reach him I kept slipping and falling over in it!... What a mess; it took me two and a half hours to clean it all up!

Another time the children were running and screaming all over the house, up and down the marble stairs with my newly-bought terracotta plant pots on the side of the landing. I kept telling them to stop running and be quiet, but too late... CRASH! I ran towards the noise, and Rocco must have slipped on the stairs and pulled over two big pots which had come crashing down; there were plants, earth and smashed pots everywhere. When I saw the mess I shouted at him, he then turned on his heels and ran with his little legs going as fast as possible to the safety of my mum's lap!

I believe that occasionally my children need to do

things on their own, making mistakes and learning from their choices so they can choose infinitely better ones. A few years ago I would sometimes interfere too much with my children's behaviour. I would focus on their negative actions and tell them off and not praise them enough when they were good. Yet this only made them focus on the wrong things they had done which separated them from their true loving all-approving self. Now I am allowing my children to be their true selves as much as possible, I am focusing upon and encouraging their good behaviour more and trying not to get so involved all the time.

When one of my children makes the other one cry, if it's not serious I leave them alone and do not chastise them; they then seem to work through their negative emotions by themselves and are happy again in a few minutes. I am trying not to bring my negative vibrations and worries to them. If I feel down I try not to interfere, only when I have shifted my vibration to a more positive feeling, and only when I have come back into alignment with my true self do I interact with them, which allows my children to stay in their natural state of feeling good.

As a single mother for these past years I am guiding them through a combination of love, discipline and setting boundaries. When disciplining them I endeavour not to let my ego overtake me by losing my temper or reacting from my past conditioning because this causes me great stress and makes me feel bad. When I do become angry, I try to stop what I am doing, breathe into the moment, feel the peace and connect with love which diminishes my anger. I then understand this feeling has been instigated by my incorrect thinking, by me being out of alignment which is teaching me that I do not want to be that volatile, reactive person any more. I want to react with love which helps my children react with love and brings love back to me! I am teaching, protecting, nurturing and cherishing my four amazing children as our children are the saviours of tomorrow, and I am making them independent, not dependent on me so they create fantastic lives and spread the *truth of love everywhere they go*.

My children are so precious to me and I know they are being divinely protected as a few years ago I remembered going through the worst day of my life when my youngest daughter Sienna went missing… It was our second summer in Ripatransone and Sienna was nearly three years old. My then partner had taken all three girls to play around at our neighbours' house which was just a little further down the valley and who had three children of their own. They were gone a long time and I was getting worried, so I looked through my dad's binoculars towards their house and could see lots of people walking around outside. Next the telephone rang; it was my partner and he was frantic, crying, "We can't find Sienna, we've looked everywhere but we don't know where she is!" My dad and I jumped into the car and raced around to the house, leaving baby Rocco with my mum and found my partner in a state of panic with sweat rolling down his temples. He told us local neighbours, farmers and now the police had been searching for her for the past twenty minutes and couldn't find her!

A sick feeling rose up from the bottom of my

stomach and I began walking around the land calling out her name, looking for my sweet baby – where was she? The whole area was a nightmare; everywhere around the house was a potential danger area, there was a massive open water well, an unsafe ruin, and sheer drops all the way down the hill. I went inside the house to find all the other children huddled together on the sofa crying and asked my two eldest daughters to tell me exactly what had happened. They said one minute Sienna was playing with them and my partner was talking to the other children's dad, and the next thing she was gone – they had no idea where she was!

I searched outside again and bumped into the children's mother, although the look on her face made my insides churn and ache. I then saw a policeman and said to him that maybe a car had stopped outside the house and someone had taken her, God forbid! Yet he reassured me and said there was no way that could have happened as it was a dirt road, along a long track and someone from the house would have definitely heard and seen a car stop. I was becoming very frightened and frantic myself because no one could find her and soon I began shouting out her name. One hour had now passed since she had last been seen and the sun was going down. I was now crying and praying to God! What if she had fallen and hit her head? What if she was lying unconscious somewhere? It was horrible I didn't know what to do and I looked at my dad for an answer, but even he was walking around in heart-wrenching disbelief…

Then suddenly I heard the most magnificent Italian words ever: l'ho trovata – *I found her!* Oh, thank goodness, oh thank you God! There was my gorgeous baby with pigtails in her hair and a big smile on her face in the farmer's arms. What joy, what relief; my partner fell to his knees crying, it was quite unbelievable! She had climbed with her little legs two kilometres up the steep hill above the house. Following a little dog she said, looking at the butterflies and picking the wild flowers for me, then sitting down on the ground because she wasn't sure which way to walk back, and that's where the farmer eventually found her in his vineyard. I took her in my arms and covered her with kisses... Love had brought her back to me and I could breathe again! The next morning the story spread like wildfire through the whole town with all the locals and some people I had never met before asking me if Sienna was all right.

Being on my own with my children has brought me so much closer to them. I am a lot more truthful when talking to them and this has helped each one express how they truly feel. I tell them about my life experiences, I explain my spiritual beliefs and I teach them to choose love and positivity over fear and negativity as I know they will have to go through their life lessons, but hopefully not as dramatically as me! I realise now that although I gave birth to my children, they do not belong to me – for they are eternally free souls. I can give them my love and guidance; however I do not seek to make them like me or want them to complete me or make them feel guilty for my failures or want them to live out my dreams because they have their own dreams and every child is unique! Life is forever changing and evolving onwards and upwards towards enlightenment with every single soul choosing its own parents and life situations to enable it to grow, transcend the ego and become *free!*

Through my spiritual studies I have found that, during childhood, children can become wounded by their early environment and social conditioning which shapes their adult behaviour because each and every one of us is a product of what we learnt and experienced when we were young. Children who grow up without love, discipline, community or meaning can become troubled, fearful, uncaring adults who take their troubles out on others. For our misguided society has created some people who think that taking and consuming everything is their right and purpose in life! They grow up thinking they are entitled to receive without giving anything in return which fuels the materialistic world view and causes dysfunctional egoistic behaviour that leads to violence and crime and which is always a cry for love and a desperate need to belong.

Nelson Mandela tells us:

"No one is born hating another person because of the colour of his skin, or his background or his religion. People learn to hate, and if they can learn to hate, they can be taught to love, for love comes more naturally to the human heart than its opposite."

Living in our dysfunctional, non-perfect world, all children at one time or another will feel negative, toxic emotions or have memories of fearful experiences which may stay trapped within the energetic pain-body and emerge later on in life as depressive moods, destructive anger, obsessive behaviours, illness or aggression; this is why singing, dancing, crying and acting out emotions are important as they help release toxic energy! If we can learn not to react negatively to this behaviour, but *deep listen* to our youngsters and react with compassion, even if we do not agree with what they are saying, and learn to focus on their true self while giving love energy to them; we can honestly nurture, guide, talk, help and love them.

Once we, as parents, begin to see that our egoic behaviour derives from our wounded *'Inner Child'* we can transform it! By opening our hearts and releasing our emotions with gratitude and forgiveness, this raises our vibration to turn fear into love and, by becoming more childlike, having more fun and not taking life so seriously, this helps to awaken our children because children imitate everything we do! Only through our example, through our kind words and actions will they be kinder too. Thus to change society's negative values, fearful beliefs and greedy cravings for more:

> "We must lead by example and change ourselves; this then changes the next generation."

Our children need physical, emotional, mental and spiritual nourishment from the adults, schools and society around them so they can feel good and transform their pain and false ego, and they need unconditional love flowing into them so they can give out love freely, which creates a loving, caring society. For children are our equals! They are fully-grown souls in little bodies and we need to talk to them as such by not pretending that the world is perfect and by not overprotecting them, overpowering them or holding them back from creating the life they want! Children are already in the here and now as they think, feel, act, dance and sing freely and instinctively from their soul and they know how to use their divine energy wisely. This is what makes them so happy, but we can't handle them in this happy state all the time and sometimes we tell them to be quiet, thus without knowing it we suppress them.

Therefore let us give our children the freedom to do what they want to do, to be whom they want to be and to have anything they want to have in life. Allowing them to express themselves in all ways and to be a magical child for as long as possible!

"For our children are our heroes and when we honour them they will honour us!"

CHAPTER 11

CONNECTING WITH MY DIVINE SELF

We are living in an unprecedented time of spiritual awakening, a time when eons of effort has brought a higher vibration of love and light upon the Earth. It will still be a school for learning our lessons and transcending our egos, yet more people are becoming aware of the love and light and realising kindness is a power that unites us together to co-create a New Earth.

JOANNE LEE PHILPOT

The children were really missing their papa as the last time they had seen him was over eight months ago when he left for London. They had talked to him on Skype, but needed to be in his arms, feeling his love again. So with his next pay cheque my ex-partner bought us five inexpensive flights to England. The children were very excited to be going on an aeroplane and to be seeing their father and I was happy to see my grandmother and girlfriends after so long. We managed to make the flight without any problems or screaming tantrums and the other passengers complimented me on how well behaved my four children were!

We had a car waiting for us at the airport, yet when my two youngest, Rocco and Sienna, first saw their papa they were a little unsure of him, as eight months is a lot of time out of a young child's life! My ex-partner became emotional and vowed that he would now come over to Italy every two months to see his beloved children. I think he was beginning to realise that he was losing his connection with them and that he now needed to be a good father. When I got out of the car and laid eyes on my ex-partner I had the most intense feeling to turn around and run in the opposite direction! I knew it was my inner guidance telling me *not to get involved with him again because he was not the right man for me.* We hugged each other; however I had lots of mixed feelings. I still felt negative towards him and I was not in any state of forgiveness.

We stayed at his shared house in south London for three stressful days; it was busy and I was not used to seeing so many people on the streets. A couple of times we argued because he tried to tell me how to bring up our children which I felt offended by as he had no idea what it was like being a single mother, raising four children on her own, on call twenty-four hours a day, living in a foreign country away from all her friends and on a low income. At night I made sure that my ex-partner and I slept in separate beds with two children each as he is an extremely sexy man and I could still feel the strong sexual energy between us! My girlfriends have all told me how they fantasised about him at one time or another, but after everything that had happened I just could not have sex with him.

We went by train to visit my beloved grandmother, auntie, uncle and cousins then travelled down to our old home town of Leigh-on-Sea to have a picnic in the park with all my closest friends and it was so good to see all of our children playing together again. It was an expensive, exhausting, fully-packed five-day trip, getting on so many trains, buses and taxis with the luggage and four tired children, yet just before we left to go back to Italy I could feel my attitude towards my ex-partner changing for the better. He said he wanted the children and me to go and live with him in London when the house was sold. I said I would think about it, yet even if he said he had changed there was no way I could ever live with him again, as for me the relationship was over. I could never live with him working nights, still partying and still womanising; if I lived that life again I would become negative in my mind and manifest an illness in my body.

Our house had been up for sale for over two years and there had been only three couples who had viewed it; because of the world recession no one had any money and the property market was not moving at all. The winter had been cold again with lots of damp and fog, and because we couldn't afford to heat the house properly the black mould had come back with a vengeance, staining our sparkling white ceilings that we had painted a while ago and which we now had to repaint all over again. I felt frustrated, discouraged and trapped here in Italy. I couldn't find a job, I had to rely on my ex-partner and his chaotic lifestyle for everything, and I was resenting the fact that the house had not been sold. I kept saying to myself, "I want autonomy, I want my independence and I want to rely on me!" I kept thinking when we sell the house then I will be free and when I move to Spain and have my retreat all my problems will be over…

But then I thought, Joanne *'you are free right now'* in this very moment! In the here and now you can change the way you think, feel and act, and therefore positively change your life, as positive thoughts and actions produce positive karma and attract good things and negative thoughts and actions produce negative karma and attract bad things. If I want spiritual fulfilment I must think consciously and feel better emotions which allow me to be the cause of my next higher experience.

Subsequently I could sense myself becoming a lot more watchful about my thoughts, feelings and words. If I did say something negative or hurtful I felt immediately remorseful about it and vowed not to behave like that again, which disperses the karma attached to it. I asked Spirit to transform my destructive delusions of anger, impatience and self-centredness. I meditated on love, kindness and compassion to oppose and purify my egoic mind and transcend my lower nature, because only by doing this would I have the freedom to connect with my *'Divine Self now!'*

I understood that I couldn't keep being attached to the past saying, "I should have done this" or "I should have done that" or being attached to the future saying, "When I sell my house or have my yoga retreat I will be happy." I want to be *happy now!* I must try not to worry about the past because it cannot be changed. I am trying to give my full attention to this Divine Moment as my thoughts and what I do now are forming my future, and because being connected to Spirit is the *'soul'* purpose of my life! In the past I was only concerned with my outer purpose and with the material things of the world. Yet the more experiences I go through, my inner purpose which is *spiritual fulfilment* is infinitely more important. I realise I am free because I have control over what I think and feel and therefore control over which direction I want my life to go. Once I feel good, my heart is open and everything I do is fuelled with love's creative power which gives me *Spiritual Freedom* because anything is possible in this amazing, unfathomable universe we live in.

Even though I realised this I would still sometimes let myself be taken over by anger, acting selfishly and thinking about all the hurtful things that had happened with my ex-partner. It was interfering with my peace of mind during meditation and every day these negative emotions were draining my positive energy and stopping the good things being attracted to me. I knew once again that I needed the guidance, inspiration and infinite wisdom of my Sat Guru, who was travelling around the world helping all people find their own *Spiritual Freedom!* I meditated and imagined that I was in his glorious presence and soon, with the help of my parents who knew how important it was for me to see my Guru, I booked a flight to London for an advanced one-day Kundalini Kriya yoga workshop.

At the workshop there were lots of people there from the time before and Yogiraj taught us three more advanced, powerful Kriyas. Towards the end he came up to talk to us and told me personally that I would benefit tremendously from one of these Kriyas as it helped one become more emotionally stable which he said I needed as he felt I had been quite volatile before! It's unbelievable what insight he has and it made me see that I needed to calm down my emotions and harmful reactions even more. I then spoke to him about the yoga retreat I wanted to open in Spain, and he said he would come and teach workshops there when it was ready. I also told him that I had been teaching Hatha yoga for eleven years and learning and practising the Kundalini Kriya yoga meditations for a few years and would like to teach them to others. He told me to carry on with the meditations, then I could do the teacher training and he would initiate me as a Hamsacharya-Kriya yoga teacher. This to me was amazing as I crave self-realisation, wanting to pass on and spread this sacred knowledge to the whole world!

Afterwards, all the helpers and lovely Indian women laid out a delicious vegetarian Indian dinner for us and we all sat together chatting and very much appreciating being with our Guru. We chant many *mantras* when we are with him and my favourite is the holy mantra:

"OM NAMAH SHIVAYA"

Chanting mantras works in a similar way to repeating affirmations. When chanting mantras over and over with heartfelt devotion, the sacred, holy words and harmonic sounds connect with the harmonic sounds of our earth and universe to transform our subconscious mind and energise and merge us with all things. Repeated repetition of the 'Om Namah Shivaya' mantra is said to cure disease and bestow optimum health on the individual. It offers protection from negative forces, reveals the true nature of reality and delivers one from the fear and constant cycle of death and rebirth.

At the workshop, Yogiraj gave an amazing talk about humanity's future:

"At this time in human history 'The Kalki Avatar' will come to Earth to balance creation. Negativity, fear and ignorance will disappear, righteousness, truth and a new mind-set will start to emerge within all people. A massive spiritual transformation will begin to happen through the entire universe, and a New Spiritual Awareness will prevail throughout humanity.

It will begin with a refining process of all people. The physical body will become strong and perfect, making a better vehicle for the expression of the spirit, and the energy body will be more important than the physical body. This improvement of mind, body and soul can then bring forth children who can compensate the spirit of God and therefore serve God better. By purifying our emotions and transforming the mind from all negativity, we will come out of the darkness and into the light!"

In the Ancient Vedic Scriptures it tells us that the Kalki Avatar is the last human embodiment of God who will come to earth destroying evil, fear and end suffering. To me this is the same as the Christian prophecy of the second coming of Jesus and the Native American Indian prophecy of The Rainbow Warriors, and means bringing balance back to the world through the Divine Feminine and Divine Masculine and raising our Kundalini which assists our ascension into the higher dimensions. Thus the Kalki Avatar is *all of us spiritual beings,* as we are all awakening to the Avatar within!

An Old Native American Prophecy:

> *"When the Earth is ravaged and the animals are dying, a new tribe of people shall come unto the Earth from many colours, classes and creeds and by their actions and deeds shall make the Earth green again! They will be known as the Warriors of the Rainbow!"*

There will be many positive and negative changes to our beautiful Mother Earth that will heighten our consciousness, creating individual self-peace and therefore peace for all, and we will come together building a *New Spiritual Race* of people. How incredible is this? I am preparing myself for this awakening and will help others do the same by spreading the word of love through yoga everywhere I go.

My Sat Guru and Babaji have shown me that the power of prayer, meditation and visualisation is astounding, and when it is performed with heartfelt devotion, faith and true gratitude for the Divine it is miraculous! A few weeks after I came back from London my dad found our big dog Rio lying on the ground too sick to move – we believe that he may have eaten some poisoned meat left by the horrible hunters. He wouldn't even drink water; we were very worried about him and said if he doesn't drink soon we have to take him to the emergency vet. I ran to my terrace, gazed into the sun and prayed to God, to Babaji to Guru with so much faith and devotion to please let my dog live. I repeated the words over and over, praying and meditating on them and visualising that he was walking around healthy. Amazingly, half an hour later my dog got up on wobbly legs and drank some water, and we were all so happy and relieved! Coincidences and accidents are important messages from Spirit and this *'message was telling me to have belief in the power of prayer, meditation and visualisation'*.

My Guru talks about Babaji, from his website;

"Babaji simply means 'Revered Father', he is the Invisible Saviour; the 'Eternal Now' who watches over the evolution of humanity from eternity to eternity till it is liberated. Babaji is the Divine Being; he is the consciousness of the universe and Lord Shiva himself."

It is so important for me to express my thankfulness to my Sat Guru and to the Divine Babaji and tell the world about them both. We can meditate on their love and constant compassion, knowing they are ever-present, protecting and guiding us all! I have been blessed to find these *spiritual helpers* for they are always with me, awakening me and giving me infinite wisdom. I cannot wait to stay at Yogiraj's Siddhanath Forest Ashram and I hope to make the trip with my children and some friends. To be in Guru's holy presence, to have my children blessed by him and to visit his Earth Peace Temple will be an incredibly life-changing experience for us all.

During these past years in Italy it feels like I have been living on my own *'Austere Ashram!'* Staying inside my house, doing yoga and Kriya meditations, studying the sacred scriptures, smoothie fasting and trying to transcend my ego – but never socialising or going out, not even for lunch or dinner! I used to like to go out and drink red wine, but now I find I can only drink one glass, maybe once a week, as alcohol really affects me. I feel that drinking heavily, taking drugs, smoking, reacting negatively and even eating meat is old-fashioned and outdated. I believe that humanity's new high will be the seeking of *spiritual pleasure,* the *giving and receiving of love* and the *alignment of our heart, mind and soul* which helps everyone feel good and to create the life they want!

"For love and enlightenment is the New Elixir of Life,
And the next in-thing to attain"

I also have to be careful with my diet; I must eat lightly and meditate before eating. The mind, body and soul are so strongly connected when I have times of thinking negatively; one negative thought leads to another negative thought then *'I'* will begin to feel bad which manifests out into my body affecting my stomach. It can also happen the other way around; when I eat something unnatural it affects my stomach which makes *'ME'* feel bad and gives me negative thoughts. When blocked, fearful, angry emotions do start to arise from my ego mind I have to remember that these emotions are simply vibrations of energy in my pain-body; they are not '*me*'. They are energy vibrations coming from my past conditioning, unpleasant experiences and collective human pain that needs to be channelled and expressed naturally, otherwise it stays within and shows up as moody, irritable behaviour just before my monthly cycle.

If I keep on thinking of a bad situation it will be played out in my mind over and over, again and again, until I become conscious of it and choose to stop it by focusing upon something I love and breathing yogically into the now. If I can separate my aware, present true self, the '*I am*' from my body and these emotions, becoming the observer and staying in the blissful still mind state, then I allow these vibrations to just be and '*I*' will not be affected by any of them. Having a healthy mind gives me a healthy body and I feel the best when I am eating lightly, performing yoga and meditation and in harmony with all things.

The first year of living in Italy was good and I had my beautiful baby boy! However these past few years have been extremely challenging, yet extremely *enlightening*. I have been going through my experiences and life lessons all with very little money, heating and even food sometimes which has restricted me and forced me in a positive way to develop *self-discipline and self-examination*. Also it has made me see that not buying so many things reduces my consumption and stops me from being wasteful and taking from Mother Earth's natural resources. The Ancient Yogis tell us some rare people have instant awakening while with others, including myself, it is a gradual realisation of the truth within. For me these last few years have been a time of learning and spiritual awakening and I am beginning to understand the reason for it all. Even my brother, who has been through many troubles in his life and has been quite difficult to live with at times, has now changed, and because of what we've all been through it has brought our family closer and we now sit and talk together, friends at last!

My parents have been fantastic, soldiering on through these demanding times, although for my mum it has been especially hard as she hasn't had a proper house to live in or make beautiful in years which has repressed all of her creativity. She worries a lot, dwelling on the negative, she does not exercise or drink enough water and her diet is not that good. Therefore she has developed several health problems and had to have lots of operations to remove kidney stones which the Italian doctors did not perform properly and consequently left her with many complications!

I think the doctors here and all around the world use surgery far too often and give out too many pills for people to take every day which lowers the body's immune system and stops it from healing itself. They are even prescribing medication for normal human suffering such as divorce, financial hardship and going through spiritual awakening; thus it is no surprise to me that the third cause of death in America is due to prescribed medication! Doctors everywhere need to wake up and stop looking through their medical books for answers. They must treat people holistically with orthodox and natural medicine and encourage them to take up exercise, drink water, eat healthily and change the way they think and feel.

I could also see the strain of these past few years in my dad, although nothing will ever stop him from sharing his brilliant sense of humour – however tough life gets he will always make you laugh! Yet one day soon when we let go of our resistance, when we have peace with where we are right now and when we are ready to allow that good feeling within us to flow, our house will be sold and we can begin our dream again, armed with the knowledge and spiritual realisations that we have all accumulated through this trying period of our life experience.

When the lovely springtime arrived, my family and I did a fantastic thing that very much enhanced our lives and our connection with nature. We asked the farmer next door to dig up and rotovate a piece of our land with his tractor so we could grow our own organic vegetables and soft fruits as the farmers around our house have shown us how easy and joyful it is to grow your own. *You reap what you sow,* which is a karmic belief, and getting the children to put their hands in the earth and planting and watering the seedlings to see the miracle of life is inspirational and healing for them – plus I couldn't wait to taste their delicious just picked organic freshness. I also made a big compost heap from all my food leftovers which gives nutrients to the earth and means I mostly have recyclable waste which does not go into landfill or take hundreds of years to decompose.

I believe that living in the countryside with its awe-inspiring scenery has really touched my soul. As I listen to the early morning cockerel, that tells me it's time to wake up; as I stretch into my yoga asanas on my terrace in the healing sunshine; as I breathe in all the splendours of nature that surrounds me and as I admire the gorgeous foal that has just been born in the field next to me – it fills me up and gives me such a sublime sense of serenity. When I walk through Ripatransone, gazing at the magnificent, never-ending view of the snow-capped mountains, it humbles, energises and excites me, giving me faith and helping me feel our subtle connection with everything on this amazing planet. I see now that I do not need to push, resist or struggle against life any more. I am remembering that I am a spiritual being having a human life experience, and I am trying to transcend my ego and to allow love to guide me. I understand that I am on earth to grow from my experiences, to be more thankful and more compassionate and to remind all people that we are here to *'create ourselves again in the highest, most spectacular way possible'*.

I then had another realisation! I had been holding on to the attachment of selling my house and moving to Spain which was creating resistance for me. I knew I needed to let life happen in its own *divine time,* to allow the process of evolution to carry me onwards and upwards, and to just *be here now* and enjoy life. I also realised that when I first started writing and saying affirmations they were always about what I wanted in my outside life, about me having my yoga retreat. However now my affirmations are about what I want in my inner life and what I want for all beings and our world. They are about me being an ethical, spiritual, virtuous person and *being of service to others.*

Now when I hear or see people suffering it touches my heart and makes me cry. I ask God to please stop all the hurt and pain in our world, to transform us with love, to alleviate our sufferings and to give us all joy and happiness. I ask myself: "What can I do to help those who suffer?, "What can I give someone to make them feel better?" and I see that by making the effort and changing my own heart and mind to have life-enhancing thoughts, caring feelings and actions of peace and goodness towards all living beings, this will not only feed their happiness but ultimately mine as well.

Every day I understand more about the power of feeling good, because when I feel good I know I am thinking, saying and doing something which is correct for me and correct for all! I am listening to the wisdom of my heart; I am realising who I truly am and I am discovering my soul purpose! For I am in the process of *'transition'* and for the first time in my life I am:

"Connecting with my Divine Self"

It was time for me to go and see my gynaecologist and have a check-up on the fibroid that had been found in my uterus months before. I felt deep within me that it had gone because I was no longer giving my precious life-force energy away into a relationship that was not enriching me. I refused to think about all the things that had happened with my ex-partner. I never went on his Facebook site again because I didn't want to be affected by any more painful, negative emotions. I felt I had released a lot of them from my pain-body with Kundalini meditations and I was a lot calmer because I had stopped thinking about what had happened in my relationship and in my past, and let it all go! Anyway none of it really mattered to me now. I was even a little grateful for all of the experiences as it was a part of my learning, my evolving and my awakening. I now feel wonderfully free and happy with myself – for I understand *the better I feel, the more good things will come to me!*

And I was right; the Doctor examined me and could find nothing, the fibroid had completely disappeared!

Then amazingly I received a phone call from a new lady who wanted to start yoga and through her my classes filled up. It was unbelievable! Women in Ripatransone began coming to my yoga classes and thought yoga was brilliant. I taught five classes a week and it felt great to finally bring money in from a job I loved doing and with little time away from the children – I knew it was happening because of my transformation. I was much more patient and peaceful when I was teaching, and taught my students the philosophy of yoga and shared my personal beliefs with them. My students have all been brought up as Catholics, yet accepted everything I taught them with such grace and understanding, even with the philosophy of reincarnation! Just to touch these ladies' hearts with the *truth of yoga and life* has been on immensely fulfilling experience for me and I thank them so very much.

It's so important for us to feel peace in every action we do; working at something we have a passion for and performing our jobs well because every job is important.

As our society changes for the better, work environments will also change; for work needs to give all people a sense of accomplishment and meaning. The workplace must offer opportunities to be a creative, caring person and to allow participation in important decisions which enhance society's living conditions and the natural world around us. People need to feel that they are contributing to the good of all and helping human development, because the more we care for others, the more peace we feel within, and the more peace will increase for everyone.

While the government of Italy has never helped me out, this mini-city of Ripatransone and many people in it have been so kind and supportive towards me, my children and my family. The Mayor has always been there for me through all my challenging situations and I now see the benefits of living in a small community as they help each other and are always working together as *'one'* for the good of the community. Our ancient ancestors lived in small tribal communities and had a deep connection with the whole of nature. But as they moved away from the natural world and began building cities, creating a *'modern civilisation'*, they forgot about their Divine Connection with Spirit, with Mother Earth and with each other, which has caused people to feel disconnected and to live alone in tiny boxes.

Yet this unnatural way of living is forcing us to search for meaning and connection again. It's awakening us to see that we must positively transform our big cities with their mass consumerism and irresponsible need for high-speed food production, and start our own conscious communities, making our own earth friendly houses, controlling our own economy and, growing our own organic food in an ecological, self-sustaining way which works with nature, not against it. These worldwide communities will make sure every person is cared for and involved in the daily production of food and living where all have enough to eat; where older generations are involved in teaching the younger ones; where all people can discover their talents and use them to evolve the community and the rest of humanity and, most importantly, where there are no elite rich or deprived poor, no egoic greed or outdated violence but where all people are nurtured and protected, living in *oneness with each other*!

Once we truly want to help others and the world, we connect and a synchronicity occurs between us. Our magnetism and the laws of karma, attraction and love draw like-minded souls together to merge into the flow of wellbeing, into heightened consciousness and into powerful manifesting where we co-create a *New Earth*! This is why I want a yoga retreat so I can create a spiritual, eco-friendly peacekeeping community that awakens others to the *Unity of Humanity*. I will let the land return to its natural state so it becomes fertile again and grow organic foods where the biodiversity keeps it abundant without chemicals and where it transforms into a thriving, edible ecosystem that is self-maintaining and self-enhancing to every single life. For if we treat and respect our planet with healing, love and compassion she will return it and look after us and our future generations because as Mother Earth-Gaia ascends, we ascend with her!

Throughout the next few months I knew for sure that I was changing because when I woke up in the mornings I felt happy! After I had given thanks, completed my sun meditations and asked for all souls to have peace and love, forgiveness and compassion and prosperity and perfect health, I began creating my day in my mind and would ask the Universe, God and my Angels to help me give love to every person I came into contact with. During the day I would remember to quieten my mind, open my heart and listen to my soul, sensing the gentle, divine love all around me. I would then be given messages, coincidences and guidance through a spiritual book I read or through an inspiring movie I watched or through having a talk with someone or through my dreams and meditations. For when I become silent, not thinking of anything, but just sitting for a while, smelling the flowers, feeling the wind on my face and not wanting to be anywhere else except right where I am in this moment. I appreciate the Divinity within me, the Divinity within others and the Divinity within everything. I feel how truly wonderful this Universe is and the wonder of us all and I realise *'Life is Divine!'*

I believe before incarnation every soul creates a *life vision* or soul purpose of what it wishes to achieve. We all choose our parents, our soul mates and those experiences necessary for our own learning and evolution, with some of us experiencing extremely difficult lessons in order to assist the evolution of humanity. When we are born into physicality, and as we grow, we may become consumed by the ego, attracting negatively, missing opportunities and feeling unfulfilled which naturally evolves us or we may *hold our vision,* attracting positively, raising our energy vibrations and feeling the majestic quality of our open hearts and minds to create ourselves as we intended.

For me, every day is a step closer to remembering my truth and living my dream! I want to create a fabulous, simple, prosperous life; manifesting my spiritual pleasures and my material dreams. However, if I am continually worrying about money I can't help others, and if I am spiritual but poor I can only influence a few. I am thinking big because I want to help as many people as possible *feel good*! I want to help you all find spiritual realisation through yoga and happiness through the laws of the universe and the secrets to life. I want you to believe in your *'Divine Self'* and to understand that *'You are Love'*, then spread this message to others.

God loves and supports us always, there are no limitations in life except the ones we think we have and there is no shortage in this miraculous world that is full of abundance. All people should have, be and do whatever they want, as long as it benefits the conscious evolvement of every living being. It's not bad or difficult to want wealth freedom and a great life; it is our birthright to live well, be happy and care and share with each other. Therefore let us be kind to ourselves by thinking inspiring thoughts, feeling exalted emotions, speaking encouraging words and performing kinder actions as they will vibrate out, affecting every person and come back to affect us. Let us be gentler and infinitely more nurturing, loving and unifying, which is the true basic nature of us all.

"I am a vehicle for God's love, light and energy
To shine through me onto the Earth for all people to
See, Feel and Be!"

CHAPTER 12

REMEMBERING MY TRUTH

I am free to just be me! In the here and now, in this present moment I choose my peaceful, blissful Self. Without regretting the past or worrying about the future, I am happy with whom I am now. In this moment I am Divine and I am creating; therefore I am free to just be me!

JOANNE LEE PHILPOT

Around May time, I received a message on Facebook from my long-lost girlfriend who is a massage therapist in Byron Bay, Australia. She had found me after sixteen years and said her one dream in life was to see Italy – so as I was feeling lonely for spiritual company I suggested she stay with me. Once my friend arrived she wanted to see Venice and said she would pay for my accommodation if I went with her. My brother wanted to come too and my parents said they would look after the children for a couple of days. I was excited as I packed my suitcase and had a feeling that maybe I might meet some kind, handsome, influential man who would be a welcome friend for a while and perhaps help me out a little! The train to Venice was an enchanting six-hour journey north alongside the Adriatic Sea with its picturesque beaches, quaint fishing boats and scenic palm trees. Arriving at Venice station we walked outside and were totally astounded by the incredible view of the Grand Canal. We then jumped onto a water taxi and were mesmerised by the old, graceful Venetian hotels and elegant houses at the side of the canal with water lapping at their doors and windows. It really was like floating around in an enchanting dream!

We got off the water taxi as it started to rain and walked through the narrow, cobbled streets with fabulous shops full of Venetian glass and incredible hand-painted masks to find our hotel. Our room was three steep narrow flights up and the view from my window was unbelievably romantic. I could see the men on the gondolas and hear them singing as they rode their passengers through the water streets; the scene was so arousing it brought tears to my eyes. When evening came we got dressed up and, after having an 'aperitivo' in St Mark's Square, then dinner we boarded the water taxi again to go to the old Venice Casino as I wanted to surround myself in decadent luxury for a change and, you never know, perhaps I would meet someone there! It's funny how things happen for a reason, because I forgot my Italian identity card and could not get into the casino; we were all disappointed but said we would go back the next night.

As we walked through the streets in the cold rain,

my toes began hurting because of the high heels that I never normally wore and the ride back on the water taxi was freezing. We arrived at the hotel drenched and my throat began to hurt; I could tell it was the first sign of a cold. During the night I hardly slept because I could not stop thinking. I felt guilty that I was spending money which I needed for bills and, as the morning dawned, all I wanted to do was go home and be with my children. I instantly renounced the attachment and desire that I had to the casino and to the kind, handsome influential man. I kissed my friend goodbye, went to the train station with my brother and changed our tickets, arriving home just in time to see my daughter in her school play.

A couple of days after coming back from Venice, while meditating in my yoga room, I had a realisation! However lonely or destitute I am, I cannot take the easy path out of my situations. I did that when I was a young escort and I visited many casinos with kind, influential, but unfortunately never handsome men and either won or was given lots of money.

I remember when I was about nineteen a friend asked me to go to one of London's exclusive members' only casinos with him, his sister, her husband and an extremely wealthy Australian man. We all sat around the blackjack table in our glamorous evening dress while the Australian gambled and, when he was finished, with a sparkle in his eye he threw everyone a chip then abruptly left. As I was cashing in my chip the teller lady asked me if I would like cash or a cheque. I said cheque please and when she passed it to me I thought she had made a mistake and put too many noughts onto the amount because it was made out for £10,000!!! My friends and I started laughing in amazement and the next day I walked out of the bank and went on the biggest shopping spree of my nineteen-year-old life!

Yet that was my past, it is not who I am today, and I could never go back there again! For I have done too much spiritual work on myself, I have raised my awareness and I could never lie to others by profaning love or lie to myself by not living my truth. I know I must go through my problems and this period of my life alone and I will never settle for second best. I want it '*All*' or nothing, I want *true spiritual love* and a *true connection of the heart, mind and soul* otherwise I will remain in celibacy for another four years! I know I am destined to meet my spiritual man and I know it will be the soulful relationship that I have always dreamed of as we will both have grown and evolved from our life experiences; we will both have more self-love and more self-peace and we will both be seeking self-realisation and thus be a *vibrational match* to each other. However for me to be a match and in order to release my ego and gain realisation, I need to lessen my attachment to fearful thoughts, to negative people, to material things and to chaotic situations.

Yogic psychotherapy is the control of thought waves in the mind; it brings the impure thoughts of the ego under our control and changes them. Our false ego craves Maya, the temporary material pleasures that cause us attachment and ignorance. Ignorance is the misunderstanding and fear of the truth and evil is ignorance because evil denies truth. When we deny the truth of God, of Love within, we deny it within everyone and everything. This then becomes resistance, leading us to look for happiness outside of ourselves and to keep on feeding the false ego personality and pain-body with more fear, negativity, guilt and material gratification which causes us stress and leads to stress-related illnesses. For we seek happiness through selfish desires; joy through deluded fantasies; love through dysfunctional relationships; self-importance through jobs we end up disliking; stimulation through frenzied life dramas; pleasure through negative obsessions and peace through the escapism of drugs, alcohol and negative images on TV. Yet all this becomes a distraction from being a kind, caring human being and is a substitute for the one thing that we all really need which is *spiritual fulfilment*!

We have accumulated so many things that soon, if we don't have self-control, our homes will be full to the brim with senseless objects that we became attached to and which brought us a brief happiness, but have now lost their meaning. The only true happiness that is permanent is the truth of the self; the eternal, immortal shared consciousness that we all are within. For nothing in this world is really ours; we come in with nothing and we leave with nothing, except our:

> "Evolving consciousness; everything comes from and belongs to the Divine"

Having a yogic lifestyle does not mean we must live an austere, poor, boring life of drastic discipline. Each and every one of us has the right to live well, have prosperity, love, good health, happiness and sufficient beautiful homes because there really is enough abundance for all on this miraculous earth of ours. If we can just have a little *self-control* over how much we eat, drink, speak, think, behave and accumulate, and are not driven by greed, but learn to share our successes and assist others to achieve prosperity, love and good health – this brings happiness to all. Living yogically means experiencing life as the human being and the spiritual being together in harmony. It means being a spiritual helper, a shining light of truth and joy, and being a human example of goodness and compassion; transcending the ego that continuously wants things all the time by having control of our mind and over our negative attachments.

It's the same for any challenging situation or problem that has upset me and I have become attached to. When I observe the nature of the situation or problem, understanding where I have contributed to them by my unloving thoughts and feelings, and once I understand that everything that has happened to me I have consciously or unconsciously attracted, I see the reason for my difficulties, I learn to take responsibility for them and I know that many are due to my wrong actions and to me wanting to selfishly win.

The Ancient Yogis tell us to surrender our will and dedicate our actions which become detachment. Surrender means to stop doing the things that get in the way of our evolutionary flow and give in to the guidance from Spirit. Dedicate means whatever we think, feel and say, let it be of service to humanity and detachment means turning away from the things that bring us pain

– turning away from the fear and staying in the love! When I surrender to love and come from my heart I am in alignment: here I let go of outside attachments which helps me step into the magical flow of creation where I receive guidance to solve any problem and where I take the correct action so that *everybody wins!*

I then performed a guided meditation by Doreen Virtue, author of my Angel Tarot cards, to cut any energetic cords of attachment to fear, worry or negativity created between people or situations from my past, and for days after I felt lighter and elated.

Once the early summertime arrived, my ex-partner flew over from London again to be with the children. The weather was gloriously hot so down to the beaches we went and, while he was teaching the children to swim and having fun with them in the sea, I realised a very important thing. That we will always be a family and even if we have other partners, it will then be an extended family! I understood that he is on his path of growing from his lessons and finding his soul purpose in life and I began to feel true empathy towards him. I know he is on a different level of evolution than I am and I have outgrown him and could no longer be in a relationship with him; however he is a kind, compassionate man.

He came over to sit beside me on the beach and, as we watched our children laugh and play, he told me that he now knows he has a problem with anger and depression and is going to anger management and to see a therapist. I thought this was great as he was finally asking for help and starting to do some self-study so he could heal and maybe awaken to his truth within. Many of us may not be ready for this inner exploration. We have the choice to begin it if we wish; if not, our spiritual helpers will continuously give us messages, experiences and lessons until we finally wake up! My ex-partner also told me that I was doing an amazing job looking after the children. He was impressed I was writing a book and he still considered me the 'hottest woman he had made love to' which made me feel appreciated!

The day came for him to fly back to London and, as I was lying in bed that night, I realised my relationship with him had been built on love, but with lots of physical lust, desire, guilt and dishonesty. It was not as romantically cherishing, as deeply fulfilling or as spiritually honest as us women and men want our relationships to be. Yet this was not a bad thing because it was allowing my heart to send out higher vibrations so that my next relationship would be all this and more. For I am attracting it to me and when I meet my honourable man we will choose to live, grow and evolve together in *love, freedom, truth and joy;* not possessing or owning one another and not expecting the other person to make us feel happy or enlightened. It will be a genuine connection of the heart, mind and soul that allows us to express ourselves to each other in a sensual, sexual, spiritual way. For it will be a soulful relationship of mutual respect, trust and intimacy where we give and receive love which opens us up to perceive each other's divinity and awakens us so that we may awaken others!

This I truly believed and I knew at that moment that my ex-partner and I had come together to learn about the feminine/masculine connection I saw the purpose of our union and the reason for the whole ordeal and how it had ended – was to awaken me! I thank my ex-partner and give him love for coming into my life, for us creating our beautiful children together and for him being a mirror so I could *'remember my truth within'*. We both experienced what we needed to from the relationship, but now it was time to let go and move on with no negative feelings!

Learning so many truths from my relationship and from my life experiences is allowing me to let go of resistance and helping me to find my-self. I will never lose my-self in any relationship again because now I am loving my-self, honouring the sacred feminine within my-self and finding my *True Divine Self* first so that in my next relationship I will not take! I will only try to give and thus create the truest, highest feelings towards the man in my life which allows us to bring peace and harmony into this world together, as there must be equality between the female and male energies that exist within all things! Women need more of the masculine positive principle which gives them high self-esteem and helps them to say no to negative people and situations, and men need more of the feminine love principle which nurtures the self and other beings and works together supporting one another.

At this inspiringly spiritual time of human evolution the repression of women is coming to an end. The *'Goddess is Rising'* and the sacred feminine is increasing once again to bring balance back to our society! There are women all over the world that have the sacred feminine; these women live from their true self and are not consumed by the egotistical mind. They are in union with the natural rhythms, cycles, divine laws and secrets to life, and they have unconditional love for all beings and are open to Divine Love Energy flowing through them which they give out to heal others. There are also women all over the world that have the wounded feminine; these women live from the ego and see life as a battle. They fight for themselves, their family, their jobs and success and may have been betrayed, abandoned or hurt which makes them feel resentment and bitterness. They feel superior over men and treat them as the weaker sex, but their soul longs to be healed.

Thus to heal the wounded feminine and become like the Goddess we have to let go of the fearful ego and realise our true identity as a Divine Loving Being that is protected and guided!

To me, 'True Equality' is when a woman sees herself as equal to men, she feels comfortable in her womanly role and allows the man to see her truth so they can truly love, connect and have a soulful relationship. 'True Feminism' is when a woman is strong, vulnerable and gentle; she knows that gentleness is a sacred human feeling which is 'strength' not weakness and that expressing emotions freely means she has a big heart and is a sign of spiritual power! Thus to heal humanity we must appreciate the unity and equality of every woman as our sister and every man as our brother! We must go within to our place of inner stillness where we fill ourselves up with unconditional love and where we learn to *love ourselves* and give out love, truth and support to the entire planetary family.

This is the *'New Love Awareness'* that is transforming the strong ego in unconscious men and the wounded feminine in unconscious women and this is why yoga is so good for both genders as it awakens and unites the Female Yin Shakti and the Male Yang Shiva energies within us all. Together *'Soul Sisters'* and *'Soul Brothers'* can honour the strength and gentleness of the Divine Feminine and the strength and gentleness of the Divine Masculine as they are but a reflection, a mirror of each other. This is the beginning of a new equality between the sexes and the start of a harmonious new world!

At this time of my spiritual journey I sense a strong connection with the Goddess which to me is the Prime Creator and the Mother of us all, and I wish to do her bidding by helping people awaken to love. I feel that I am finally honouring the feminine within myself and within all women and that I am honouring the masculine within myself and within all men. At last I feel forgiveness towards my ex-partner for all his wrongdoings; yet the more I think about it, the more I see that there really isn't anything to forgive because the experiences he has brought me have spiritually evolved me and therefore I am thankful for them. I really do want the best for him now and not because he is the father of my children, I want him to be the true man he is inside and I will try to help him be this in any way I can.

I also feel that living on my own and abstaining from sex these past years has been incredibly beneficial because it has cleansed and purified me from my past. I have been transmuting my sexual energy by not channelling it on sex where it becomes dissipated into the lower chakras, but through my Kundalini practices my sexual energy transmutes into spiritual energy which opens and speeds up all seven chakras to give enlightenment. Sex energy is very powerful; it gives us a strong desire for action and when we control, transmute and sublimate this energy we become driven by it and can creatively direct the mind and manifest our thoughts into physical reality.

One day I was watching a talk online that my Sat Guru Yogiraj Siddhanath was giving on sex, Kriya yoga and marriage, and he tells us:

"The practice of Kundalini Kriya Yoga transforms sexual energy into spiritual energy and the pure passion energy of sex can be used and transformed into the pure passion energy for Enlightenment and God. Marriage is union between man and woman, and woman reminds a man where he comes from, the woman is:

'The Divine Mother, the Source of Creation man was born from'

And the man reminds the woman where she should go:

'He Leads her to her Heavenly Father, to God'

You must have reverence for each other as the manifest forms of the Goddess and God. When you feel the desire for sex, joyfully fulfil it then carry on with your spiritual lifestyle. Sex is the most natural and sacred prayer! When it is in a loving, evolving relationship it is transcending."

I believe when either a man or woman is deceitful in a relationship it gives their power away and sex made without love is not wrong but depletes our energy; both hinder people from reaching enlightenment. Sex made with love replenishes our energy, helps us to awaken and gives us exquisite erotic feelings. It is the magnificent way we express our love for each other and it's the celebration of every life! *Sex is Sacred!* It is the miracle of creating human life and the magnetism and attraction we feel for each other is our *Spiritual/Sexual Energies Embracing*, two becoming *'One'* which merges our individual soul consciousness with Universal God Consciousness.

From the book *The Tenth Insight* by James Redfield:

*"Sexual union is a holy moment
In which a part of Heaven flows into the Earth"*

Making love opens up a doorway for Divine Love from the spiritual to manifest into the physical, as the incredible experience of orgasm is the feeling of divine love and bliss that exists within the spiritual world all the time. Therefore the act of lovemaking must be respected, honoured, spiritualised and made into a harmonious ritual with all of us cherishing it, loving it and doing it as much as we like! The practice of *spiritual sex and sacred sexuality* is a form of physical communion between the female and male or between the same-sex partners (as all ways of loving are virtuous to God) which raises our vibration and is so wonderfully enlightening and transforming.

This is *Tantric Sex* which combines sex, love and meditation. It awakens the Kundalini, our spiritual/sexual energy, by raising it up the spine where it opens and connects the seven chakras of both individuals and unites Shakti energy with Shiva energy in *Samadhi*. At this Divine Moment our chakras connect to the chakras of the entire solar system becoming one with the Universe, God and two individuals become a whole person and experience the *'Ultimate Orgasmic Ecstasy'*. Thus bliss through spiritual sex and bliss through enlightenment is the same thing, and all of life is the sacred rhythm of giving and receiving this Divine Love/Light Energy.

The Indian Guru of Tantra, Osho, tells us:

"Tantra is the science of turning ordinary lovers into Soul Mates. It can transform the whole earth; it can transform each couple into soul mates. It has not yet been used. It is one of the greatest treasures lying there, unused. The day humanity uses it a new glow will surround the earth; the earth will be aglow with a new love."

I was very sexual for many years but felt unfulfilled and knew there was a much more soulful, passionate, spiritual, transcending side to making love! I now live with excited anticipation that when I meet my true partner, my soul mate, my twin flame, we will perform spiritual sex and create beautiful sensuous music together that joins with the rapturous harmonic music of the universe! Women and men of the world let us not put all our precious energy into meaningless sexual exploits or the acquiring of more meaningless things. Let us not lose our *true self* in any relationship again, but let us live in the now and put our energy into soulful relationships, honouring our *Divine Feminine* and our

Divine Masculine by sharing sexual pleasure with those who love, cherish and respect the *sacredness of our revered Mind, Body and Soul*.

For our soul is always in a natural state of pure loving presence, this is our natural state of being which is *'unconditional love'* and this divine state of love gives us peace in every moment because God is this present moment! When I look at my children and animals they are always content because they live in the here and now. When I walk on the land through the aged olive trees that symbolise peace, I can feel the trees and flowers are always in a perfect state of stillness, they are always in a present, blissful state of *'being'*.

I am trying to live with conscious awareness in every moment because here I am happy and fearless which releases my ego and allows me to manifest my spiritual and material goals. I am trying not to think of what could have been in the past or how happy I will be in the future because when my attention is in the past or in the future I am in relative time, not in the absolute now; thus I create time on my body which ages it! Only when I am mindful in this instant do I feel *'One with Life and One with Spirit which is Eternal and Timeless'*. For our negative ego lives in relative man-made time, but our Spirit Soul is the everlasting truth which dwells only in *Eternity!*

"The past and future are an illusion of our minds, only this moment exists!"

I have to remember that this moment is the only moment to be kind, thankful and giving. Now is the only time to unify and see the divinity within me and within all living beings which has always been there waiting for us to have realisation of it and discovering this eternal truth is the *New Evolution of Consciousness and Compassion* for one another. I must understand that I need to be happy and blissful now; to appreciate the journey, the place and the moment that I am in now! Even though it's difficult and it's not where I want to be, I chose it and I am here! Therefore I have to let go, make peace with it and be in alignment with now because '*now*', this divine moment is where everything happens:

"The miracle of life is now, Now is All There Is!"

Yet the past couple of weeks of me trying to transcend my ego and seek peace in the moment had been extremely difficult; I seemed to be fighting with my old self, not wanting to let the negative false ego side of me go. I was moody and irritable all the time, shouting at my children and having no patience for them. I kept saying "I want change! When is my real life ever going to happen?" It had been five years since my partner had left for London and since I had started writing this book, and six years of going through my challenging experiences. Furthermore, because I had not been able to create my yoga retreat, I was not conversing with spiritual people and I felt isolated, abandoned and cut off from the rest of the world living in this rural area of 'Italia'.

I was bringing up four children and doing everything on my own – cleaning the house and cooking breakfast, lunch and dinner every day. I was trying to pay the enormous bills with hardly any money and I never got dressed up or went out for dinner which every woman needs to do, to give her a break and to make her feel good. I had been celibate the whole time and hadn't even had a cup of coffee with a member of the opposite sex, let alone gone on a date! I wondered where my strong spiritual man was to help me with the heavy shopping, to entertain the children for a while and to take me out for a romantic dinner. I took solace in my Angel Tarot cards, but even they were predicting gloominess! I felt good for a while then I felt bad, and I'd had enough of living this way; I wanted to feel good constantly and it appeared as if I had come to the end of it all...

Things became so unpleasant that I could not stay with my positive, balanced state of mind and I felt it was an accumulation of everything bringing me to this point of crisis! My lower back went out of alignment, hurting continuously and my second Sacral chakra seemed blocked, which means lack of emotional support and unbalanced feelings. I seemed to have lost my *true self* once again; I was engulfed in my pain-body and I became dreadfully stressed and lonely. Therefore I decided to step up my meditations. When I awoke in the mornings I bathed, did not eat, got the children off to school then went straight to my yoga room to sit in meditation for an hour or sometimes longer trying to find peace… Yet that blissful still mind state, I touched fleetingly.

I understood the truth in my mind that I am always *connected, always one with love, one with God,* but I just did not feel it in my heart. I was distracted and could not stay present; for even though my soul longed for freedom, love and peace I could not oppose my dark, fearful feelings. That night when all the children were asleep I prayed to Spirit to give me truth and presence and to give me realisation of God within. I was so emotional, I prayed and prayed and cried and cried until I eventually fell asleep.

A few days later, after dropping the children off at school, I came home, looking through some of the inspirational films that I had downloaded the night before and was spiritually guided to watch the fantastically moving true-life film *Conversations with God* based on the books by Neale Donald Walsch. At the end of the film, God says to him:

> *"Do not feel abandoned for I am always with you, I will not leave you, I cannot leave you for you are my creation and my product, my daughter, my son, my purpose and my Self. Call on me therefore wherever and whenever you are separate from the peace that I am. I will be there."*

I cried so much through that harrowing film as it touched my *soul* and then at the end when I heard those words, something shifted deep within me. I closed my eyes and took some yogic breaths which brought me into presence. I performed one of my Kriyas raising the Kundalini energy up the spine and I chanted OM. After twenty minutes or so, while immersed in that blissful state of awareness, I felt my energy heightening and I sensed a peaceful light all around me. I began *remembering my truth within* and had an intense feeling of love for myself! The stress seemed to release from my mind and body effortlessly and I was perfectly content in the present moment. Amazingly I didn't feel alone any more, *I felt one with the divine* and knew for certain that God was here as a part of me, inside my heart all the time.

I'd had a shift in consciousness and a shift out of my ego and I'd been given the truth and presence that I had asked for. In those enlightening moments I had the most momentous realisation of my life!

As long as I seek the *light* I will have *shadows*! My shadow side is my unconscious fears and the dark parts of me that I do not want to acknowledge or show to other people. I see that the shadow is only my lower nature limiting me and blocking my light and when I cut the energetic cords of attachment it helped me to delve into the darkness, releasing and transforming my fears, letting go of the things that do not serve me and loving who I am now! For the more I choose love over fear and bring light where there is darkness in this world, the more brightly my majestic light shines, which becomes a beacon for others to see through their darkness. I see my shadows are only a projection of me not believing in myself, of me not '*loving myself*' and that *self-love is self-realisation and the realisation of God, of Love within!*

I was crying tears of joy as it was all so poignant and I whispered to myself, "So this is what it feels like to live wisely in every moment." All I have to do is go within and remember my truth; for eternal truth only comes to me within the *sacred silence*! Now when I feel challenged by life or things get difficult, I stop what I am doing, close my eyes, breathe into the present moment to feel the higher me within, to feel the shared self within and to feel the love within. Here I surrender my will, bringing that peaceful feeling into every thought and I dedicate my actions for the good of all which sets me free to *"Just be me!"*

I am happy just to be my truthful honest self, to just be the new me in this divine moment of now, and to change my *self-centred reality into a Spirit-Centred Reality!* I know I am being divinely guided by my Angels, Spirit Guides and the Goddess to have self-love and peace, as peace is my present state of mind undisturbed by good or bad situations and self-love is my happy state of being which heightens my magnetism and attracts all the good things to me. For I am a human/spiritual being that is always evolving, creating and becoming ever more loving, ever more compassionate, ever more truthful, and ultimately ever more spiritual.

Osho tells us:

"Don't try to force anything.
Let life be a deep let-go.
God opens millions of flowers every day without forcing their buds"

As I go outside into the glorious summer sunshine, I take my shoes and socks off and walk barefoot on the ground to receive the love energy of the earth which heals my body and raises my vibration. I see the abundance of our organic vegetable garden that we planted just a while ago, I pick the delicious lettuce and spinach leaves and the crunchy cucumbers and juicy tomatoes to make my lunch. I see the profusion of succulent fruit on our trees which I pick for my children when they come home from school. I walk over to the field next to me to stroke the little horse and its mother and am amazed at how spiritually aware they are and I can't stop kissing, cuddling and laughing with my children and animals, and feeling the profound love connection with their souls!

At long last I am learning to appreciate and become humble from doing the simple, modest things which help me to stay down-to-earth and unassuming and which are attracting the bigger things to me. I am trying to be here now where all the power of the universe lies; where I am forgiven for the mistakes of my past; where all miracles happen and where I learn to love me, love all beings and thus create my *Divine Life*!

"I am connecting with everything
I am the life within everything
I am Peace
I am Presence
I am Compassion
I am Love
And I am so truly thankful for it all!"

CHAPTER 13

SALVATION

In the realm of the Absolute all Souls are part of the One Eternal Super Soul. This Supreme Being wants to experience everything and so separates into individual Souls to be born into the realm of the Relative. Since that time Man and Woman have been deeply driven to merge once again with whom they truly are; to merge with their Spirit Soul, with their Soul Mates and with the Oneness and Divine Love of the Collective Consciousness of Us All

JOANNE LEE PHILPOT

It was nearly the end of August, and before the children went back to school I decided to take them to Sorrento to stay with their lovely nonna, the mother of my ex-partner. We took the morning bus to Naples for five and a half hours and then drove along the dangerous yet breathtaking coastal road to the little town of Meta, in the region of Campania, close to Sorrento. When we rang the bell of nonna's house, she flung open the door and cried 'Mio Amore' – 'my love' – then proceeded to engulf us with hugs and kisses. Walking inside, the scrumptious smell of southern Italian pasta cooking on the stove whet our appetites and I knew the delicious Mediterranean salad on the kitchen table had been made just for me! As we sat down to eat with my ex-partner's step-papa who had been our builder, all my blame towards him over the bad workmanship on our houses and terrible use of finances dispersed! He was so old and I only felt love for him, although when he cut the head off the cooked chicken and started sucking its insides out, I understood how 'old school' he really was!

That night the children and I delighted in stroking and playing with nonna's ten beautiful cats and we all slept in the king-size bed that she made up for us. In the morning, because it was so hot, we packed up our beach bags to go swimming in the sea. As we walked through the old winding streets of Meta, we passed numerous sweet-smelling groves of the biggest lemons we had ever seen, until finally walking down a steep flight of steps to gaze at the crystal-clear blue waters of the Mediterranean. The beach was of rough, black sand due to the volcano eruption from Mount Vesuvius in 79AD which devastated the town of Pompeii and left black volcanic sand throughout the region!

In the evenings we would go for a pizza 'Napoletana' made from tomatoes grown on the volcanic plains south of Vesuvius and buffalo mozzarella that melted in your mouth or we'd jump on the train to Sorrento which is one of my favourite places ever! I cherished strolling through tiny, narrow street markets selling traditional white cotton clothes and Italian aromatic spices or browsing through shops selling lacquered wooden music boxes that played the song 'Torna a Surriento' – 'Come Back to Sorrento'. Before we got the train home we would take a seat in one of the outdoor cafés in the elegant Piazza Tasso. Nonna would buy the children the finest 'gelato' (ice cream) and I would have a glass of 'limoncino', a lemon liqueur made from the intense zest of Sorrento lemons. It was such a delightful little break and we were sad saying goodbye to our loving, eccentric nonna!

When we arrived back home my two eldest daughters both entered the singing competition in Ripatransone again. Incredibly Gina won first prize this time, Lola came second and in school and around town everyone told them how 'fantastico' their voices were! A while ago I became worried that I could not afford to send my children to all the activities or take them out to the places they wanted to go. However now I see that what could be more wonderful than being brought up in such peaceful countryside, close to animals and the pretty sandy beaches, as well as staying with their family in London, Rome and Sorrento. I knew my children would look back on their idyllic childhood with happiness, seeing it as a colourful and enchanting time. It made me see that as a single mother I was doing a brilliant job because my children were turning out to be good, kind, talented people!

When olive season arrived, the whole family had fun harvesting our fifteen olive trees which were packed full with overflowing abundance. My dad worked in the olive oil factory again where he pressed all our olives and made enough organic oil to last throughout the coming year. After Christmas in late January it became extremely cold and around the beginning of February, on the day that my ex-partner flew over from London to be with the children, it began snowing, heavily. The snow was so bad his plane was diverted to another airport near Milan. He then took a bus for six hours to reach our seaside town of Cupra Marittima and because all transport had come to a standstill in the area, he had to walk uphill for an hour through thick, freezing snow in the middle of the night to reach our house!

The next day the snow came down even heavier. It was a metre high on my terrace, the view from my window looked like Siberia and it was dark, eerie and I felt completely isolated and a little scared. Ripatransone was on National Italian News three times as it was buried in snow; the reporter said it was the worst winter for eighty years, and it was even snowing on the beaches! We got 's*nowed in*' again, I couldn't get to teach yoga, the children were off school, and I was so glad that their papa was with us to help keep them all occupied.

The owner of the olive oil factory had given me an old wood burner which I placed downstairs and, after years of living in Italy, we realised it was the cheapest way to heat the house. We bought a little wood but mostly we used all the excess hard olive husks that were left over from pressing the olives. They burnt well and my dad said he could make bricks out of this reusable, eco-friendly fuel that would be good for the environment – I couldn't believe that the Italians had not thought of manufacturing it as there were lots of olive trees in Italy! Yet our house upstairs was freezing because we couldn't afford to run the radiators, and all we had were two paraffin heaters to keep us warm. So we put all the beds together again in one room and I made sure they were warmed up with hot water bottles every night.

It took the town a very long time to grit the roads which are especially dangerous in Ripatransone, but of course this is Italy and everything gets done in its own '*Italian time!*' My dad and ex-partner had to drive the car into town with chains on the tyres to get some provisions. They drove slowly through the snow, barely seeing the road and skidding all over the place which was not very good when you're looking out of the window down a sheer drop! It was an unbelievable experience as I had never seen so much snow in my life! Yet, it didn't get me down and I was actually laughing because I knew that all things pass away and nothing stays the same.

> "Relative life is forever changing,
> only the Divine Life within is everlasting"

As we were snowed in and couldn't go out, I retreated to my bedroom to practise yoga and, as always, read my books and I began contemplating humanity's suffering. Our precious lives on Mother Earth are for the expansion of peace, love, joy and compassion; however throughout history human beings have always suffered. Suffering means being in alignment with our false ego where we feel bad and joy means being in alignment with our true self where we feel good and where all things are possible.

Everyone suffers and through my own pain and suffering I am reminded of what others have had to go through which makes me feel compassion for them. The hurtful things and negative situations I have experienced on my path, the emotional agony has opened my heart and made way for spiritual discovery; thus my suffering is teaching, transforming an awakening me.

Suffering and being hurt dissipates the ego, it takes us out of our comfort zones and frees us from our limitations. Therefore let us see suffering as a way of evolving because painful events are a justification for spiritual growth and they help us see that there must be a better way to live! Some of us may blame God, other people or outside situations for our sufferings in life, but it is always identification with the fearful ego mind and attachment to the pain-body that causes us to suffer. Thus to end our suffering we must be the observer of our pain by stepping out of our fear and identifying with love, this is our *Salvation!*

> "We have been addicted to suffering!
> It's time to be addicted to love"

Spirit has a miraculous purpose for each individual life and Spirit has given us the same creative mind power as God our creator. However, it is easy to see that, with the overpowering collective ego and its selfish greed and unrelenting desire for money and power, we are unconsciously reacting in the same old negative ways which leads to more suffering. Furthermore, with our wrong misguided creating, we have formed ourselves and the things in this world in an inferior, disuniting, primitive way!

I believe many indigenous societies are not *'primitive';* they are advanced because they are *'old cultures'* that understand the oneness of the natural world. They have aware minds, open hearts and infinite wisdom from thousands of years of caring, respecting and giving back to the earth! It's our so-called *'civilised'* society that is the primitive one because we take, we consume and we kill without thinking of the consequences of our actions or how we are destroying our environment and exterminating the cultures and species that we can learn from to reconnect with nature and each other again.

Yet if we can stop perceiving the world and ourselves in a distorted, damaged fearful way and begin seeing the truth of love within everything, using our creative mind power positively and responsibly to transform ourselves and attain peace within, we will not be so concerned with egoic moneymaking endeavours, but will desire the experience of our soul which gives us spiritual pleasure. Then all will understand that being gentle and kind and *taking care of every life – is true strength!* This will finally be the end of suffering and the beginning of a liberated humanity, for this is not a world of fear, this is a world of love and this is our New Consciousness of the Heart that is emerging at this time and *awakening us all!*

Later on in the year, two astonishing things happened that gave me true belief in my power as a creator and in my spiritual helpers. The first thing was that my ex-partner could not find any work in London. He was very depressed and upset about it and for many months he was not able to send me any money or come over to see the children. Consequently things became exceedingly difficult for us here in Italy. I can honestly say that having no money or little food in the fridge, and especially when you have four children to look after, was one of the most distressing and destitute experiences I have ever lived through. I called up the European Commission because, as a British citizen and a member of the EU, I thought I would be entitled to some financial help for my children. They told me to talk with the Italian authorities again who then told me that I was entitled to nothing from the Italian government. I could not believe that this country which boasts of family values does not look after women and children!

The money I received from my yoga classes was not enough to pay my bills so my parents and the children's nonna with their tiny pensions began helping us out and of course my Angels helped too! Although it was financially the worst time ever, I tried my best not to feel resentful towards my ex-partner because I understood that carrying resentment around in my heart destroys my wellbeing and eventually manifests health problems. I sent him love and focused on my spiritual and material goals which made me feel good and I decided to do a magical ritual on the next *new moon* to bring me success and abundance!

New moons are a powerful time to set intentions for things we'd like to create, attract and manifest in our lives and an important time to let go of the negative things that do not serve us any more, thus making room for the new. Once it was night-time and the children were asleep, I set up sacred space in my bedroom by lighting my incense and smudging myself with sage to clear away any negative energy. I created a sacred circle on the floor with my favourite crystals, feathers, Tarot cards and candles in the centre, and I asked the Goddess/God and the Angels for protection. I lit the candles and performed one of my Kundalini Kriyas which opens my chakras and brings mind, body and soul into alignment and I chanted OM which heightens my energy vibration! Next I wrote down and said my intentions out loud and visualised and meditated on them with love; I felt the feeling of having them and I opened my heart and was thankful to receive them. At the end of the ritual I asked that this magical work be done in the correct way and for the good of all, so be it! Then I closed the circle.

Over the next few weeks I realised that due to my recent shift in consciousness and to my new feelings of self-love and most significantly to the ritual I had performed, I started to feel extraordinarily positive! I became happy and optimistic, and even my children told me how calm I was. It was incredible because the better I felt, the more good things began happening. People I had never met before began helping me out, money came to me from different sources and even the local town community started giving me boxes of food every two weeks. We were just about paying our bills and just about surviving!

Then the next astonishing thing to happen turned out to be the greatest time in my life when I was helped by my Angels! My beloved grandmother in England died of old age... We were all heartbreakingly upset and I missed her comforting lovely voice on the phone terribly. Yet amazingly, I found out that my sweet, generous grandmother had left me a large sum of money in her *will and I would receive it soon!* I could not believe it because things were getting worse for us. We had no money to buy wood for the fire and had to pull up all the old outside decking which we burnt with our olive husks to keep warm. Our only car had broken down the week before and we had to walk uphill and thumb lifts into town. The children all desperately needed new clothes and new shoes, my fridge was barely working and my computer was making funny sounds and on its way out too. It was a true *MIRACLE!* Right at the time of my life when I needed money the most, it miraculously came to me. I then knew that I didn't need to rely on my ex-partner because it's all in my thanks that I give out to the universe which makes space in my heart to receive abundance.

> "It's my positive loving vibration, intention and magnetism that attracts all things to me"

The Goddess/God and my Angels had heard my intentions and felt my vibrations, and the magic power of love had manifested them into my life! I saw that by not resenting my ex-partner, but by 'girare la pizza' turning the pizza as the Italians say and sending him love, this had dissolved any resistance and brought me into alignment which allowed me to become a pure channel for the laws of attraction, karma and love to work. I realise now that I have control over the events in my life and that *I am safe and I am blessed!* If I don't resist or get in the way of my conscious evolution, Spirit will bring everything to me, as I have come full circle – being one with God in the absolute world where I remember and know everything, then being separated from God in this relative world where I forget everything and know nothing! However now I am coming back to the joyful oneness again. I am remembering my Godliness as the Divine Creator of my own life experience and I am completing the *Circle of Life!*

I am following my bliss and my inner guidance, and when I *think and feel with the wisdom of my heart and soul* this empowers me to choose my own personal outcomes. For *I am the Source*! I am creating everything with my thoughts, feelings, words and intentions and this is my freedom, my truth and me falling in love with my-Self!

> "We project what we feel
> and what we feel we become"

When the English solicitor put the inheritance money into my Italian bank account it was an astounding feeling and it only deepened my belief that my children and I were being *'Divinely Protected'!* Throughout the following weeks I went on many shopping sprees. I bought a fantastic second-hand Italian car for a great price and I made an important decision. If I stayed in Italy all my inheritance would go on living and soon run out. If I went to live in Spain I would have to rent an apartment, pay for bills and food for me and the children, and if I didn't find enough work there I would soon be in the same poor position as Italy. I just could not take that chance and I could not go through what I had been through these past few years again!

Therefore we would go to London and rent a little house in a green, leafy suburb. It would be challenging and I would be taking a giant leap of *faith;* however, being a single mother of four children I knew the English government would help me out. I'd receive child benefit again and the children could go to English schools and do their singing, art and drama. I could teach yoga and focus all my energy into getting this book published, and my parents would stay behind in Italy to sell the house which I hoped wouldn't take too much longer!

Our property had been up for sale for nearly four years. We had lowered the price so many times to try and sell it that we had lost a lot of money and therefore did not have enough to create our retreat together – only enough money to buy one house. Also the architect sent us a letter after nearly eight years wanting another six thousand, five hundred euros for work he never did on our second house that was never built! My dad was furious as he knew we were being taken advantage of because we were English and because we couldn't afford to take the arrogant architect to court. There was no way out, and we had to pay him otherwise he would not sign the papers which in Italian law permit the house to be vended; the money would have to come off the sale of the house, leaving us with even less.

This prompted me to contemplate my parents' situation. They needed a house to live in and wouldn't be able to get a mortgage or pay rent on their small pension. So I decided that because I am younger and can start again, I would give all the money from the sale of the house over to my mum and dad.

As soon as I made this decision, I had a realisation! My share of the money had been made from negative earnings when I was a young escort and deep down in my soul I knew that letting go of it would purify my karma and open my heart so I could receive true abundance. I also knew that with all the secrets and truths I had learnt and, most importantly, with God's help, somehow I would have the means to create my yoga retreat again. For this *Spiritual Awakening, this Love, this Wisdom and this Truth I had been given on this journey was worth every lost euro!*

Napoleon Hill tells us:

*"Every adversity, every failure, every heartache
Carries with it the seed of an equal or greater benefit"*

For I have the creative power within to make my dreams come true and I know I will manifest Magic and Miracles in my life! I believe it will not take long for me to have my spiritual community and maybe the powers that be want me to create my yoga retreat in London – to help all the stressed-out people there. My retreat will have a large yoga studio where I will create weekend workshops so people can learn 'Yoga, Meditation and the Secrets to Life and Eternal Truths'. We will be eco-friendly, growing organic fruit and vegetables in fertile forest food gardens; we will create our own energy and not over-consume, and we will learn to get more out of life by using less! As our society is so fuelled by money that all goods are made for a profit and therefore not made to last; once they break down they are thrown away and new ones have to be made, and this uses up energy and depletes the world's resources! We need to change our social conditioning and make goods that can be recycled, upgraded, are good for the environment and made to last. Once we learn to simplify our lives and become more resourceful and once we learn to use the vibrational frequency of love to become self-creatable, we are boundless and can manifest anything!

At this time of my life I feel I have finally stopped talking about the same old story of my past problems and difficult situations as I know that putting my attention on them will only attract the same things back to me over and over again. Now I am telling a new story of how I wish my life to be and of the spiritual person I am so this is attracted to me! When I began this Italian journey I wanted enlightenment selfishly, for myself only; however now I want enlightenment for the sake of everyone. I want all beings to have self-realisation, self-love and oneness with each other!

As I become self-realised I see the purpose of every relationship is to join. I see all living beings *as the same Immaculate Self, as the same Spirit and as the same Light within* which is an ancient eternal truth. As I become enlightened I am in a state of self-love, forgiveness and presence. For living in the now *is all there is*; being in the now with peaceful awareness and feeling oneness with my soul and with the whole universe. Realising the self is the God and Goddess within all life-forms – it is love in its purest state. *I am That I Am! I am the Life, I am the Love and I am the Divine Soul Consciousness within everything. There is no separateness; there is only One Supreme Being, One Eternal Super Soul who placed a part of its Self inside every living being; this is who we are and this is our SALVATION!* Jesus said to everyone:

"The Kingdom of Heaven is within you"

An *Awakened Soul* brings a heightened consciousness of love into this world, and therefore enlightens others and transforms the environment with their simple spirituality and their peaceful state of *'being'*. They are recognised by a certain strength, beauty and purity that emanates from them. They are strong because they are perfectly relaxed, having found union between mind, body and soul and do not waste their energy with destructive thoughts, words or actions. They are beautiful because their face and movements reflect the inner and outer bliss and harmony of their life. They are pure because they live in the here and now, receiving vibrations from the environment and the collective ego, then transforming these vibrations and redistributing them as love energy, *giving to all people and all situations lovingly and unconditionally.*

"Radiating the Infinite Light through their Infinite Souls"

Buddha, Christ, Krishna, Babaji and Muhammad are this and the divine plan is for every soul to become like them! As human beings we have the potential to destroy ourselves and our planet or to become like Buddha, like

Christ and like God which is humanity's salvation. The Buddhists tell us that having a human life is rare because only by being born a human do we have a spiritual opportunity to attain the highest perfection and not revolve on the cosmic wheel of birth and death again! Therefore, let us all love and appreciate ourselves, each other and this remarkable planet that we all share, and let us not waste this valuable human life experience, but create ourselves anew and make a better world together.

I know it's not easy to transform our minds, open our hearts or to live in this peaceful, blissful way all the time because we are constantly being pulled back into negative thinking, selfish desires, deluded fantasies and material attachments. In fact to live in peace may take many lifetimes, but if we can live this way for one minute a day, that's one minute of pure, powerful peace and eventually that one minute will become five minutes and slowly this will transform us to live in *peace and bliss* for most of the time. I believe that one day I will be enlightened, hopefully within this present life!

Although I am not there yet. I have long periods of being aware, being in the present moment, and sometimes whole days of thinking inspiring thoughts and feeling completely connected to all of life. Then something will happen. I may let a situation, place, person or thing affect me or allow my worries and fearful shadow side to overwhelm me which pulls me away from my feel-good place. All this feeds my pain-body and leads to continual fearful thoughts until I consciously stop worrying, breathe yogically and come back to the present to feel good once again.

It's a learning process to move away from my fearful thoughts before they produce more and I do this by focusing on the first loving, intuitive thought which comes from my heart and soul and putting my attention on trusting in the Divine, even when things go wrong – trusting that if I calm myself and ask for guidance, a solution will present itself! Because everything is OK, because all things are working out in the correct way and for the good of all, and because with every choice I make I am creating my *own conscious evolution.*

Life is truly incredible! I feel blessed to be here at this time of universal awakening and not missing a single moment of the tremendous transformation of:

"Humanity evolving into Divinity"

At this time I feel content (well when I'm staying in the love that is!), I feel gratitude towards God/Goddess for helping me to cultivate kindness towards others. I thank Spirit every day for helping me feel self-love, and I thank the Divine Babaji and my Sat Guru for awakening me with yoga and meditation. It's truly amazing because even my ex-partner has begun a Transcendental Meditation course! He now meditates for twenty minutes every morning and is a lot calmer and happier with himself. Every day I am remembering to allow my Spirit Soul to take control, every day I am remembering that everything has to happen in its own Divine Time and every day I am remembering that God already knows what I want and guides me there quicker than I ever could! This is spiritual mastery which is achieved by being the *Master of my mind, the Master of my body and the Master of my Life!*

I see my experiences are not that bad when compared to other people's around the world and I feel privileged to be able to practise yoga and to have good health. I understand that no lesson or experience is ever wasted or in vain; in fact the messages I receive through them awaken me. They are very powerful provided that I grow and evolve and do not stay stuck repeating the same lessons over and over again. When I look back on my youth nearly thirty years ago, I see why I took drugs and alcohol, why I worked as a topless dancer taking dollars for tips and why I gave myself away as an escort… I had to go so low, so that I could raise my vibration and lift myself higher and higher out of it all. I had to go through the bad, unworthy stuff so that I would know myself as *worthy and good* and become the *Spiritual Yoga Teacher* I am today!

For now I am respecting and blessing that person I once was and letting her go. Now I am realising that the most important lesson I had to learn in life was not to forgive myself for all the things I went through, but to understand and accept that they were self-created by me and a necessary part of my journey towards me loving me! This profound understanding has allowed me to make *Peace* with my past, make *Peace* with myself and want to bring *Peace* to the world!

I sometimes can't believe the things I did when I was young; I have changed so much it's like it happened to a completely different person! However my destiny was to come to Italy, to purify and cleanse myself by being celibate for so many years and to go through these challenging yet extremely enlightening experiences which are stripping away my ego and healing my body, healing my mind and healing my soul. Now I am becoming a *Healed Healer,* because only when I heal myself can I truly help and heal others who have been wounded by their life experiences.

Now I can bless every so-called bad thing that I have ever been through because to me they are not bad! They are the greatest times when I moved beyond my attachments and spiritually evolved the most – thus I see them as my *Individual Salvation*!

All of us need to go through our challenging times and rediscover self-love in our own ways because we all have our own understanding of what is right and wrong according to our sacred point of view, and because everyone changes, spiritually evolves and awakens in their own Divine Time. Now, because I understand the wisdom of blessing every so-called bad experience, I shall try not to condemn another's path as good or bad. I shall try to respect their choices and see them as important experiences that will evolve them; otherwise they wouldn't have chosen them. Furthermore, I shall try my best to help dissolve people's negative illusions of guilt, unworthiness and fear by making them laugh and showing them the soulful, playful, creatable side of life!

For our soul has to experience all things so it can evolve higher and higher in every lifetime! In our world of duality there is evil, yet without evil we would not know good; in our world of duality there is delusion, yet without delusion we would not know truth; in our world of duality there is suffering, yet without suffering we would not know joy; in our world of duality there is fear, yet without fear we would not know love and in our world of duality there is chaos, yet without chaos we would not know *Creativity and Peace! Duality is the way we express our free will, it's the Yin and Yang of Life, until we become Enlightened and embrace the oneness which means the End of Duality, and God's Heavenly Plan.*

The world may seem to be in chaos, but *'chaos'* is a learning process – out of the darkness we will evolve into the light. So let's have faith and hope, and remember that the miraculous progression of evolution is always moving us towards the truth, towards the light, towards the love and towards our *Collective Salvation!*

We don't need to go to an Ashram in India to remember this or to learn yoga, meditation and the path to salvation; we can all experience these things from our own homes and within our own families! When I first came to Italy I did not feel like a yoga teacher and I was not ready to open a yoga retreat. Only now do I feel like a *true householder yogini, only now do I feel like a true teacher and only now do I understand that this is my spiritual purpose.* At last I am becoming my vision and creating myself in the way I have always dreamed because my purpose is God's purpose, and God's purpose is peace within us all!

Through my years of teaching I see that it's not about being special or admired. It's all about giving love, deep listening and being humble, as my children and yoga students have taught me that I learn from every person I meet and everyone is my teacher! I also see that praying is not about asking for the things that I want all the time. *Real prayer is the feeling of love and love is real magic!*

Praying is a way of directing thought and transmitting love energy in a powerfully spiritual way. It means to be in a blissful state of meditation, in the sacred silence of now where I am not asking for anything but where I understand that *every moment of life is the prayer*! It's where I am heightening my magnetism and attracting the light and higher beings to me and where God inspires me to act as a *Divine Messenger of Love,* manifesting healing and inspiration for all to hold the *New World Vision of Peace together!*

Yoga is my path to self-love and self-peace and yoga is bringing me home! The yogic path can be for everyone, just look at me; even after going through these difficult years in Italy, I am still on my journey towards enlightenment, I still believe in my dream and if I can do it then *anyone can!* You just have to believe in yourself, find a true Guru or teacher and make time to practise. For me, being a yoga teacher means living the middle path, having moderation in all things and merging my humanity with my spirituality which unites the space between *Heaven and Earth!*

Yoga and meditation can benefit us throughout our entire lives; dissolving stress, keeping us fit, strong and healthy; bringing positivity and harmony to the mind, body and soul and giving us unity with each other. We must not think that because we are getting older we have to slow down or take it easy as this creates weakness in the mind and brings entropy to the body; let us all strive for a healthy, loving mind and attain a healthy body always! I know when I'm eighty-five years old I will still be standing on my head and when I am ninety I will still have muscular arms and legs, and *feeling good* because:

> "We are only as young or old as we think and feel ourselves to be!"

If I want to be a spiritual yogini and have union with that Divine part of us all, I have to think, feel, speak and act like a spiritual person. I have to tell myself often, "How would a yogini think? How would an enlightened being feel? How would a self-realised human speak? How would Divine Love act?" I have to *'Be them now, so I can become them now'* and then I knew once and for all:

> "Yoga is not my hobby, yoga is my SALVATION!"

CHAPTER 14

PEACE, LOVE, UNITY AND EQUALITY

*Love never dies; as our consciousness continues
So does our love for each other,
Through lifetime after lifetime and beyond.
Become one with love and dream your life into being.
There is only love, there is only God
And you are both!*

JOANNE LEE PHILPOT

I see why I ended up in this quiet area of Italy with a half-built house in the hills, struggling to bring up four children on my own and going through all these challenging experiences. It's because I asked for self-realisation and to be a spiritual yoga teacher so of course it was never going to be an easy journey, and I needed the silence, solitude and willpower to do it all in! I brought my children and family over to a place which we had never seen before. We all leapt out of our comfort zones and into the unknown to take the most difficult path; yet this path has set me free to feel *peace and love* within.

Peace is such a patient evolution! Yet when I look back at the chaotic person I was a few years ago, I see that I am making progress because I can feel my peace staying with me for longer moments throughout my day. As I am letting things happen without resisting them, I am surrendering to love and allowing the process of evolution to carry me forward and I am remaining in my feel-good place a lot more. I know sometimes I will be pulled into a negative place in order to grow and evolve; however I am learning to appreciate that uncomfortable negativity as it causes me to seek positivity. For our purpose on earth is to evolve from our challenging experiences, egoic relationships and unpleasant situations until we:

> "Bless our negativity as it causes us to
> know our Divinity"

Many of us think, "When I find a better job then I will be happy, when I find a different lover then I will be happy, when I move to another house or country then I will be happy," but these things will not make us happy as we take our problems and ego with us wherever we go. All through these last years in Italy I thought that selling my house, moving to Spain and creating my yoga retreat would give me joy. However I was wrong, for it's not the end result that gives me joy; it's *enjoying* this journey I have lived through!

It has been an extraordinary experience, a remarkable, precarious, unfolding journey of remembrance and understanding, and a spiritual journey inward of acceptance and realisation. This path has been my *'Rite of Passage'* into being a strong, kind, spiritual woman and my *'Initiation'* into yoga and finding the truth of God, the truth of love within which to me is the most important undertaking we can make in life; everything else is temporary and transient, only the Spirit Soul is Eternal. I bless every moment of this journey, for it is where I found divine love and I believe that on my next voyage I will find physical love to assist my *'Sacred Quest into Wholeness'*.

This journey has taught me that self-realisation is not so difficult to attain, for it is our natural state of self-love and it means to be in this divine moment which is the only moment for loving, giving and having peace of mind. This is our *greatest experience* where we choose only love-based thoughts, words and actions which help others to become more loving too. Being self-realised gives us an understanding that we are the creators of our own life experience and that the universe and all sentient beings are forever expanding, moving and evolving, towards the light and towards oneness and spiritual freedom.

Self-Realisation, Enlightenment and Love Awareness is our absolute truth! It means to have no problems, no worries and to have a change of heart and create ourselves in the likeness of goodness and in the likeness of love, which is the highest purpose of all!

We don't have to sit in meditation for hours to become realised; it's the bringing of peace and presence from our meditations every day that gives us harmony in our lives. This blissful awakened state is our birthright and makes all normal activities in life become joyful. We do not react to good or bad things, we just accept everything *as it is* and live from our pure being. When we stay in the love all our senses become heightened. We hear, feel, speak, see and touch the truth of life and know that, in every moment, miraculous things are happening all over the world. We realise *life really is Divine*! The sweet smell of a flower becomes intoxicating; the simple sensation of the sun on our skin is so pleasurable; listening to the waves of the ocean becomes like a beautiful, inspiring song, and as we look up to the heavens we experience its celestial perfection which mirrors the celestial perfection within our own hearts and souls!

"Love Awareness is Salvation, Nirvana in our body now!
It's Heaven on Earth now!"

All through the month of June I had been looking at houses to rent in different areas of London and phoning up lots of English estate agents. Eventually I found a tiny three-bedroomed house in Bromley, South London that I could afford and, with the help of my ex-partner's references, I managed to secure it by sending the deposit and first month's rent over. I didn't know anybody who lived in that area; however it seemed lovely with lots of green parks, great schools and a fantastic shopping mall. By the beginning of July I had packed all of mine and the children's belongings into boxes which would go with our heavy furniture on the removal van after we left. I planned our journey to England on the route map and decided that we would drive up across Italy then through Liguria, the Italian Riviera, and on to the south of France to stay with my gorgeous girlfriend in Cannes who would spoil us for a few days. Then we'd drive through France and jump on the Channel Tunnel train up to London.

The time came for the children to say farewell to their Italian school friends and I was sad saying goodbye to my only English friend because I would miss our yoga sessions and spiritual talks over macchiato coffee in the local bar. My heart ached at the thought of saying goodbye to my parents, brother and all our animals and it felt absolutely awful to leave them behind. When the day arrived for us to leave I filled my car to the brim with all our personal possessions. Our beloved dogs wagged their tails madly as we gave them a hug and I think they sensed we were leaving. The children and I kissed and hugged my mum, dad and brother with all of us crying tears of sorrow at our parting; for they are our closest family and our best friends and we would miss each other dearly! When I got into the car my eyes filled with tears again and I had the biggest lump in my throat – but I knew I didn't have a choice, I had to go!

We set off and frantically shouted and waved goodbye to our loved ones, then driving past the next-door neighbours' cantina, we shouted and waved goodbye to them. Once we came to the end of the road we looked up towards our little town Ripatransone, that had been such a big part of our lives for the past eight years, and we shouted and waved goodbye to the town. We then got onto the 'autostrada' and drove for many hours; I listened to music and my four children watched movies on their tablet in the back seat. I made lots of stops along the way for coffee, lunch and bathroom breaks and got lost a few times as the Italian road signs were disastrous! As we reached the region of Liguria, the Italian Riviera, I got off the main autostrada to drive along the picturesque coastal road and gaze upon the dramatic scenery of Cinque Terre – five fishing villages – and the stunning beaches of Sanremo, which gave me a brief nostalgia for the Riviera delle Palme. However the moment we drove over the border of Italy and France the children and I cheered because we were so relieved to be out of Italy and to leave all our troubles behind!

I felt excited as I was moving forward on my spiritual journey and on to my next material adventure and I did not feel fearful or unworthy any more as I was living my truth and healing myself. When we refuse to live our truth or to hear the truth people tell us or the truth a book shows us because we know it will hurt and challenge us to go to our darkest place within, our healing is postponed! We must face it all, then once the pain is faced, healed and released it will never come back!

For the first time in my life I know who I am and who I will be! I am a self-realised yogini and spiritual teacher; I am an insightful author and engaging philosopher; I am a love activist and a peace revolutionary for the people; I am a loving mother, daughter, wife and sister and a wonderful friend and helper of humanity, and finally I am grasping what my ego is!

My ego is a tool which I use for spiritual growth! The ego's fear aspect helps me to acknowledge my fears so I can release them and it assists me in letting go of the people, places and things that do not serve me any more. Ego awareness allows me to understand the reason for challenging situations and negative experiences, and to see the Good or God in them all. This is the Law of Contrast which launches my improved desires out into the universe and forces me to ask for all the good things. So instead of reacting negatively to my challenges, I transform old habits and past conditionings and react consciously with positive feelings to create the life I want. For it's not what happens to us, it's how we deal with it and how we use it to become either a victim of our circumstances or a creator of them!

Finally I get that I am a vibrational being and the universe attracts back to me the physical equivalent of the emotions I vibrate out. *Emotions are Prayers*! This is a Secret to Life to realise that I must come from my heart, from a feeling of love first before I take any action, then all outcomes will be happy because when I allow love to be in control instead of the fear-based ego, I always get the best experience! It's all about me feeling good with my true self now, me being in alignment with my sacred heart now and me understanding the divine laws of karma, attraction and love now so I manifest abundance and one day *dream my yoga retreat into being!*

Abraham-Hicks tells us:

> *"The path to financial abundance is simply an emotional path!"*

I see now that I have always been one with Spirit, but relative fear caused me to create the false ego self which separated me from my true divine self and to forget who I was which brought me unhappiness. My ego wrongly thought that I was segregated from God, inferior to God, and could never attain to be like God because of my so-called *'bad sins'*. However, I have not *'sinned'*; I have merely made mistakes through my incorrect thinking and simply lacked self-love! The Immaculate Divine Essence is not separate from us… *it is us!* We are created in its image, we are God expressing in this physical body, and we must let who we are within become our true identity. Love Energy seeks to create through us and we must allow it to by accepting that life responds to us! It's time for each and every one of us to recognise ourselves as the *Magnificent Love Creators* that we really are.

Marianne Williamson tells us:

"Love is what we are born with. Fear is what we learn. The spiritual journey is the unlearning of fear and prejudices, and the acceptance of love back in our hearts!"

All of us need to think in connection with whom we wish to be, say words that reflect whom we wish to be and act in accordance with whom we wish to be because being this attracts more of being this until we naturally become this person all the time! This is why we need to go within, to feel self-love and to be in the peaceful moment of now where we tap into prana. Only here do we know ourselves as pure creative energy, only here do we get into vibrational soul alignment to effortlessly attract perfect health, prosperity and spiritually evolving relationships and only here do we listen to the truth of our soul and heart, not the false cravings of the ego mind and body.

> "For the body is always doing things,
> but the *soul is always being them.*
> We are not a Human Doing, we are a Human Being
> Do nothing, be everything!"

Writing this book and going through my experiences has helped me to awaken to my divine self. I hope this book inspires you on your journey and may it help to awaken the *divine within you* because awakening and being a compassionate, giving person in every moment is the righteous behaviour, spiritual work or *'dharma'* in Sanskrit that your soul initiated before you were born and that you came to earth to do. Only then can you begin God's work which is to help everyone else *'awaken'*. Love is our divinity and our divinity is the answer to all our fearful problems, destructive thoughts and any terrible situations. Love dissolves our judgement, guilt and unworthiness and our divinity sets *us free!*

> "We are never alone when we are
> connected to Divine Love
> One day we will live together in happiness
> Believe that you are Divine for your
> Divinity is your Salvation!"

This is the natural process of *Divine Evolution*; all things must evolve or pass away. Humanity cannot go on the way it is! We can't keep living in this selfish, destructive, negative, egoic way which is destroying us and our world; we are in a crisis and we must wake up and stop making the same mistakes of our past... Yet I could see that this is the Yin-Yang of life because, as I have proved with my own life lessons and personal crises, they pave the way for *transformation!*

If we can let go of our judgements, condemnations or how many times we have been hurt in the past; if we can remember not to lose our temper when someone does something bad to us, but understand how wrong it is for us to be angry towards them because a true spiritual person would not want to harm anyone; if we can realise that the people who hurt us are helping to transform our minds and to develop forgiveness, kindness and tolerance; if we can see that we are all a mirror to each other as deep within we all have more love to give or more fear to release, and if we can learn not to waste any more time or energy in doubt and worry or miss out on life by regretting yesterday and stressing about tomorrow.

Instead if we can just feel a little self-love and a little self-peace; if we can surrender to our soul's guidance and focus on what we love now; if we can give freely from our true selves and support others in finding their truth within and if we can come together, accepting our differences by healing the problems that separate us. We will enhance our 'Common Unity – our Community' as Divine Loving Beings which leads to *peace, love, unity and equality* with each other, and we will see what is working to improve our lives, what is helping us to consciously evolve and what new innovations are assisting us in creating a peaceful, united world.

> "This is our greatest time to change physically,
> emotionally, psychologically and socially
> And to advance spiritually, politically,
> technologically and environmentally"

Humanity is realising that it needs a change in values where our concerns are to protect all people, all animals and all trees and plants, rather than the accumulation of money, power and material things. It is recognising that we need a global resource-based economy that eliminates scarcity and creates abundance for all; that allocates the world's resources to the needs of the people, giving them food, shelter and medical care and that preserves every species of life and protects the natural world.

For we know in our minds we must move forward with meaningful politics and community leadership where we govern ourselves, making our own decisions and giving all people a just democracy where everybody wins. For we know in our hearts we must create new systems for education, health, law, energy and spirituality which empower every individual. For we know in our souls that we must generate socially responsible businesses, corporations and investments which improve our world and bring all people, all creeds and all nations together. This will create an ethical economy and thus a virtuous humanity that produces human beings who fulfil their spiritual purpose and material goals and are therefore happy, caring and of service to others.

Once people are not constantly worrying about physical survival and basic needs are met, it becomes easier for them to work at something they enjoy and to raise their awareness and contribute to society. Once we begin healing the negative ego mind that keeps us all in a chaotic unconscious sleep and commence our *conscious awakening,* this will transform our world and bring harmony to us and to our future generations.

There must be a Global, Ethical, Ecological, Loving, Compassionate and Truthful:
"SPIRITUAL TRANSFORMATION AND SPIRITUAL REVOLUTION"

"For when we awaken to love, to God in our hearts, We recognise the divinity within every woman and man This is humanity's Divine Nature and our New Spirituality and Our true Universal Religion!"

This is my Sat Guru Yogiraj Siddhanath's 'Mission Statement'

"Humanity is our uniting religion
Breath is our uniting prayer, and
Consciousness is our uniting God"

My Guru has talked of this *new evolution of consciousness* which is happening to people all around the world with negativity, fear and ignorance disappearing, and righteousness, truth and kindness giving us a *new spiritual mindset.* For the solution to the world's problems has to be spiritual! All people must have self-love and self-peace so they can have a healthy mind and a healthy body and thus behave differently by thinking, feeling, speaking and acting in a more loving and unifying way which is our natural state of being then passing on this positive love energy to others, which is the evolutionary flow that awakens us all. We will then remember that we are part of the collective consciousness of every soul in creation and that:

> "We are a part of each other,
> We are one planetary family and a one world community,
> We are one sacred heart and one sacred soul
> For there is only one life on Mother Earth
> And it is shared by all living beings
> This is our Liberation!"

There is only *One Supreme Being* working through all beings and when we realise this truth we will no longer be able to make war upon each other, as we will be making war upon ourselves! For when we harm others, we harm ourselves and when someone we love suffers we suffer too. *Conflict cannot exist if humanity has Unity;* this is the *New Unity Consciousness* that gives us freedom from fear and true trust in each other where we *give* instead of *take* and where we yearn for community and work together in peace. In the midst of this new spiritual *trust, peace, love, unity and equality* we will not need so many military bases in the world. We will stop producing so many weapons of war and nuclear weapons of mass destruction which cost trillions, depleting the world's resources and making the big wealthy corporations and banks even richer and therefore able to control us with fear, poverty and inequality even more! But we will use this money to give all people a good, decent life.

> "For there is only one race of people on this planet
> The Divine Human Race"

Each one of us needs spiritual fulfilment and we will all have a spiritual calling sometime in our lives; for it does not matter where we are, what we do or who we are with; eventually we will all follow our hearts and fulfil our purpose of bringing peace and love into this world!

At long last I felt I was beginning to fulfil my own spiritual purpose as I had settled into my new life in England amazingly. I was teaching yoga classes, yoga weekend workshops and studying to become a Kundalini Kriya Yoga teacher. I was bordering on becoming a vegan after being spiritually guided to watch a documentary called *Forks over Knives* and I read an astounding book called *The Ancient Secret of the Fountain of Youth,* where I performed its five Tibetan postures every day and I could see they were reversing my ageing process! All my children were at brilliant schools, my three daughters were singing and acting and my boy was child modelling. I loved London and its multicultural society, and after living in such a rural area of Italy it felt right to be in a big city with forests around the corner and brilliant neighbours that helped me out with the children. I was connecting with my inspirational girlfriends again; I was meeting lots of new spiritual people and I was creating my community, my tribe! I sensed that due to the heightened vibrations I was giving out I would soon attract my spiritual man and create our Yoga Retreat.

Finally my parents sold the house in Italy! We were much relieved because we were missing each other terribly; however it was the most stressful, negative experience for them. Due to the crazy Italian law, before they could sell the property they had to have electric, plumbing, gas and land work certificates which the builder should have sorted out years ago but never did. This held up proceedings and cost a small fortune which had to come off the sale of the house again! Then when the day came to move out, the English removers sent a van to collect all their furniture, but it was too small. I must have called up the furniture removers twenty times to get them to send another van over and when that one arrived at ten o'clock at night it was still too small – consequently they had to leave lots of possessions behind, including a box of my treasured books!

My mum, dad, brother, three dogs and one cat then drove across Italy, through Switzerland and along the German/French border without any delays and slept in the cold, damp caravan they were towing for two nights. Eventually they reached Calais and at customs the animals' passports were checked, but unfortunately the Italian vet had forgotten to sign my cat's passport! My poor exhausted parents had to leave customs and chaotically drive around Calais for hours trying to find a French vet to sign the passport and of course pay out more money. By that time they had missed the last train through the Channel Tunnel to England and it was raining torrentially!

It was incredibly frustrating, they were so close to home, but no, another thing to go wrong. They had to park in the customs compound which was the safest place and try to sleep through another night in the caravan that was now leaking!

Early next morning my mum anxiously called me up to say she did not have enough money in her account to get the car, caravan and animals through the Channel Tunnel because the money from the sale of the house had not cleared! I could hear the desperation, fear and stress in her voice and she was close to tears. I told her not to worry and reassured her that we could use my rent money as my inheritance had run out months before. As soon as I got off the phone I immediately went online and transferred it into her account. Later on that day my dishevelled parents, brother and animals arrived at my house in Bromley and it was such a joy to see their faces! In the evening our whole family went out for a delicious Indian dinner as my parents had not been to an Indian restaurant in nine years and we had a wonderful celebration.

The following night around 4am, my mum woke up in such agonising pain that my dad and I had to rush her to the local emergency department. She then stayed in hospital for the next three weeks with an extremely serious kidney infection caused by two large kidney stones which the Italian doctors had not picked up on the numerous scans they had performed previously. I truly believe the stress of selling the house and the cold, damp, exhausting journey back to England had brought on my mum's infection. Yet I knew our Angels were looking after us because if it had happened on the drive back through Italy or France, it would have been terrible. I think my mum sensed something was wrong with her, but she held on until she arrived in London where she knew she would get properly looked after by the NHS!

What a stressful, worrisome and chaotic time for her and for us all! I had my dad, brother and all the animals camping out in my little house so every day we could drive to see my mum in the hospital. I couldn't do my regular morning yoga practice or meditations and because of all the stress and worrying about my mum I had a few too many glasses of wine with my dad and brother which made me feel even worse and gave me painful knots in my shoulders. I realised if I wanted to help my parents, I had to detach myself from the negativity, turn away from the worrying fear and try not to get so involved with the stressful situations of their lives. For I have no control over how people think and feel and therefore no control over what they attract to themselves. I saw that instead of being lost in my lower ego mind, I had to be aware in my higher loving heart and pray/meditate/visualise for my parents to be surrounded in positive love energy.

It takes practice to stay in a still mind state of presence because we are constantly being pulled back into thinking. Yet by going within to that quiet, alert fourth state of consciousness we bring peace into every cell of our body and into every corner of our mind which gives us spiritual awareness. For our lower ego mind dwells in the physical dimension of fears, worries and attachments, but through meditation we see the light of truth and realise this illusory realm is false, delusional and meaningless. Only thoughts created by our higher heart and soul in the spiritual dimension of love are true and meaningful, and because only *Love is Real!*

I then had an important realisation! Due to all the suffering my mum and dad had been through these last nine years, I felt that they had lived out a lot of past negative karma, and just like me I told them things would turn around. Two days after my mum got out of hospital, my dad took her house hunting on the south-east coast of England and, amazingly, the second house they viewed, they loved! At the estate agents' office my parents put their offer in and, when the agent told them it had been accepted, my mum cried! After everything they had been through, after the never-ending challenging and depressing Italian experiences, finally, good things were beginning to happen. I was so happy for them both and sensed all the stress releasing from my shoulders.

A few days later at my Kundalini Kriya yoga training, my teacher asked me to demonstrate some of the Kriyas. I was nervous because I hadn't been practising enough, but the moment I began performing the first Kriya I felt calm. I remembered everything I had been taught and my voice seemed relaxed and precise. My teacher was pleased with me and said I would make a great Kundalini Kriya yoga teacher. I then had another realisation! All the stress, negativity and worry that I had been through were actually beneficial for me because I was accepting these fearful feelings and recognising them as the contrasting parts of me that were not yet awake! They were only my shadow side overpowering me and trying to convince me that fear is greater than love. I saw my fear and negativity as poisons and that being free from them would keep me young and healthy; I saw my shadows and lower nature as an illusion that I could transmute with the light and I saw that through the chaos I was learning to be peaceful. My favourite philosopher and poet Rumi tells us;

*"Being a candle is not easy;
in order to give light one must first burn!"*

Every day I am remembering to let go of the fear and stay in the unlimited power of love and every day I am remembering to come back to my present place of peace. For the Secret to Peace is in this Divine Moment! Where the past cannot hurt us, where the future has no hold over us and where our false ego, judgement and unworthiness do not exist, but where we can begin again creating this world anew in the most loving way possible.

As we bring balance back to the world through the Divine Feminine and Divine Masculine we feel concern and empathy for other beings; we want to alleviate their suffering and have responsibility towards every life on earth and to our future generations. Once there is a positive shift in people's consciousness and the segregating craving for excessive out of control wealth, disproportionate amassing of profits and hoarding of material things which cause debt and unhappiness are reduced in society; once we realise that we can live out our spiritual purpose and our material goals by sharing our abundance and having unity with each other then crime, violence, aggression, scarcity and starvation will be greatly reduced.

We can then be presided over by small peacekeeping communities and an *Awakened Human Race* that understands if it advocates fair trade and equal opportunity, if it combines wealth, profits and resources globally and if it teaches all children spiritual values and helps all people and all species to live good, decent lives, it will ultimately help itself because everything is interconnected. Nations can then come together for the good of all, resolving the world's problems peacefully through unity consciousness, and creating a *One World Union* where all people have more food, more security, more prosperity, more freedom and more love! For it is only through our collective consciousness that mass evil or mass good is created on earth, so it is through our own self-awakening and conscious thinking that together we can transform *Hell into Heaven*!

It's up to us individually and collectively, with the power of our new spiritual awareness, to create and manifest change in our world. We do this by personally volunteering to uplift and befriend the young, old and oppressed; by helping and empowering poverty-stricken families and communities; by convening awareness to every job, profession and occupation we do and by leading by example and practicing the power of giving and the power of love, this will naturally effect positive change in others. We can personally intervene against big business exploitation, government injustices and environmental pollution worldwide, which will create the intelligent, responsible use of science and technology, and allow Mother Earth to *self-balance* and *renew* again!

There are awakened people all over the globe that have formed conscious communities and created social, political, ecological and spiritual change. Once people see that change is possible, we can all unite and form one powerful movement which will transform us all! We have the choice, so let's choose the greatest, grandest life-evolving choices because to be human means to work together in unity for a better world!

For this *Global Transformation* to happen there will be some increased instability as our wrong, negative thinking and outdated beliefs come to an end and we transcend our selfish taking ego; yet as old systems break down, this makes way for better methods of living and being to emerge. Humanity can then evolve into an even greater spiritual consciousness that embraces every life. We will see the incredible creativity, truth, goodness and synchronisation that have always been inside us, waiting to be realised from the beginning of time, and we will know beyond doubt that there has never been any lack on earth, *only lack of love within ourselves.*

The more we live by the Laws of Karma, Attraction and Love, the more we move into blissful alignment, where our Kundalini energy rises up through the chakras towards Heaven, where our magnetism heightens and where we give out the right signals to attract physical and spiritual love, success and prosperity, and perfect health and longevity! Good actions produce good influences, so to help ourselves and all people create celebrated, peaceful lives we must be virtuous and loving in everything we think, feel, say and do because the universe is always reacting to everything we give out and because we are a part of the whole universe.

> "If we want to manifest peace in the world,
> we must all strive for self-peace!"

Therefore let us all begin telling a new story! Let us all share the dream of *Peace, Love, Unity and Equality* because the more people who believe this, the more it will spread and create *Humanity's Ascension!* Salvation can be ours now by accepting and forgiving each other, by treating each other as equals and not competing with each other, and by seeing the *Divine Love* within each other. We will then rejoice in the oneness and trustfulness of every brother and sister, of every single soul that is joined and together again! We do this with our empathetic feelings, empowering visualisations and meaningful meditations, with our euphoric prayers, sacred rituals and divine ceremonies, with our passionate music, heartfelt singing and engaging art, and with our truthful films, ingenious drama and inspirational books. We join together and change the collective consciousness for:

> "We are the Love/Light Workers
> that we have been waiting for!"

Yet do not be despondent, thinking that this can never be achieved, because if we do become enticed by our ego or attached to the materialistic things in this world or consumed by our fear, doubt and unworthiness; if we do believe the lies that humanity has been led to believe for so many years, the lies that we are separated from love and resources are scarce so we cannot share them or trust others; these lies have turned into the evil service to self which is selfishness and can only be overcome by service to others which is selflessness. This is the New Spiritual Awareness that will set us all free because in the end *God, Spirit, Love is Unavoidable!*

Each and every one of us are *Dreaming of a Divine Life* and I felt mine was finally here as wonderful things were happening to me and my children. My daughter Gina was in a singing competition on TV called "The Voice Kids". My Sat Guru initiated me to teach Kundalini Kriya Yoga and I became a Hamsacharya! And I had met a man who like me was transforming his ego and in service to others and I thought maybe he was My One True Love!

We can all have a Divine Life now, if we can transcend 'Maya', which is the illusion of our limited awareness and become infinitely limitless, we can dream the new vision of peace and love into being. For it all comes from the way we perceive; if we perceive the world through the eyes of the false ego, we see only conflict and negativity and cannot have peace or love, but if we perceive the world through the loving eyes of God, we see goodness and positivity and have peace and love now! Once we open our cosmic unified heart and see correctly, we see the truth, we believe the truth and we act upon the truth to change the world view from *ego-centred separateness to Spirit-Centred Oneness.*

We are Powerful Creative Beings who are now experiencing a physical life so we can bring pranic love/light energy from the spiritual into the physical; so we can stay in the love and manifest our heart's desires; so we can evolve and ascend our consciousness from the third dimension into the fifth dimension and recreate our world, thus forming a New Enlightened Humanity and a New Golden Age. Therefore let us bring the Goddess, the Sacredness and the Divine Presence back into our everyday lives because, with every passing year, more people are awakening and dreaming a *NEW EARTH into BEING!*

Let us celebrate being alive and have fun playing the game of creation and let us unite our hearts, our minds and our souls forever in love. For love is the most powerful energy in creation. For love is the answer to everything. For love eliminates all negativity and through the power of self-love, all pain is transformed into awareness, understanding and peace.

"Our purpose is to remember our love within and
bring love into the world!
You are Love and you are Divine!
Let us all save the world
With Divine Love"

A Prayer and Affirmation:

THANK YOU SPIRIT FOR GIVING PEACE, LOVE AND SELF-REALISATION TO EVERY SOUL ON EARTH SO THAT WE MAY KNOW THE TRUTH OF YOU WHICH IS THE TRUTH OF OURSELVES!

OM
NAMASTE
PEACE AND LOVE TO YOU ALL
JOANNE LEE

EPILOGUE

ETERNAL TRUTHS AND SECRETS TO LIVING A DIVINE LIFE

Wake up early in the morning to gaze at the sunrise, allowing its pranic love energy to purify your mind, revitalise your body and bring joy to your Soul. Give thanks to the Universe, God and Goddess for all you have and will receive. Ask that all living beings have peace and love, forgiveness and compassion and prosperity and perfect health, then meditate and create your day in your mind. Surround yourself with as much natural beauty as possible by going for walks, jogs or playing sports in blissful nature, out in the fresh air which invigorates you. Take your shoes and socks off and walk barefoot on the ground to receive the energy of Mother Earth which heals you. Stop and sit for a while being present, breathing in the prana from the trees, feeling oneness with the rushing water of a stream, appreciating the beautiful flowers in your garden and just celebrate being alive!

Let's all smile, laugh and be playful a lot more! Smiling and laughter are infectious and the more you smile and laugh the more others will smile and laugh with you. You can help conserve

Mother Earth's resources and stop the suffering of animals by cutting down on your meat and dairy intake or better still become a vegetarian or a vegan. You can have a wholesome Sattvic diet by eating nature's delicious fruits, vegetables and energy foods and drinking lots of pure energising water. Be Self-Sustainable, Ecological and Resourceful by growing your own organic fruits and vegetables on your land, garden or terrace and make your own free energy to run your car and home so you never have any more bills! Turn off mainstream TV and News and watch inspiring films and documentaries from the internet and read spiritually enlightening books. Do what you love, be in a job that makes you feel good, performing your work selflessly and give spiritual awareness to every occupation and profession.

You can keep yourself pure and healthy by being in a loving, nurturing relationship that helps you to grow and evolve or you can be on your own and abstain from sex for a while, transmuting your precious sexual energy into spiritual, successful energy. Practise being happy throughout your day; anytime you think a negative thought, STOP, BREATHE, FEEL AND BE AT PEACE, then think a positive thought. While waiting for something, be patient, be aware and be present! If you do feel lost, fearful or depressed, bring yourself back to your feel-good place by listening to music that makes your heart soar or dancing away the negative energy or by painting a wonderful picture, taking relaxing baths and massages or doing yoga or sports or anything which arouses your passion and gives you joy. If you have any pain, injury or illness in your body close your eyes, breathe yogically, open your heart and bring Divine Love Energy into the exact location of the pain; the love will transform the cells and atoms to heal you. You can also send healing love energy to others who are suffering.

Accept life 'AS IT IS,' even the things you do not like, accept them and do them in a peaceful way. Surrender your will and control, allowing Spirit to guide your life. Let go of attachments by turning away from the things you do not love and focusing on the things you do love. Remember it's not about how others think of you; it's how you think about yourself. Transform your fear-based thoughts into love-based thoughts and give love to all living beings, situations, places and things. For what goes around comes around; this will give you good karma in the future. Change your material desires into spiritual desires by practising non-attachment to wanting more meaningless things, and do not become so affected by positive or negative outcomes but… BE THE CAUSE OF YOUR EXPERIENCES NOT AT THE MERCY OF THEM! Meditate and bring healing prana into your body and be silent so you can listen to the messages and coincidences your Angels, Guides and others are giving you. Before you make any decisions, ask the Divine for Enlightenment and be thankful for what you will receive.

Forget your past and begin again, meet others only in this present moment because everything is 'Forgiven in the Divine Miracle of Now!' Ask yourself often, "How can I uplift others today?" "How can I uplift myself today?" "Have I been virtuous in my thoughts, words and actions?" "What have I learnt from my experiences and where am I, am I in the past, am I in the future or am I One with Life in the timeless now?" Every person you come into contact with try Deep Listening with compassion and focus on their true self while uplifting them with love energy; this heightens their awareness. If you react negatively towards others, feel remorse about your behaviour and vow only to REACT WITH LOVE from now on because this brings LOVE back to you! Let go of fear, as there is nothing to fear in this universe; there is only LOVE! Your mind becomes sick from incorrect perception, from seeing the delusions of the ego as real, therefore when you heal your mind with love your body will be healthy! Forgive everyone and react with forgiveness as forgiveness is our SALVATION!

Understand that through every negative experience you are evolving for the better. Always remember you are the Divine Creator of your own life experience, and you dream your life into being; for life is not happening to you, life is responding to you! So put your attention on your highest dreams and inner purpose, creating your material goals and the spiritual person you truly are because your beliefs can manifest anything! Remember to say and write your positive affirmations and conformations in present time without wanting, otherwise you will be wanting forever. When you wish to attract something, ask and give thanks from your heart, then focus on it with love and faith, and visualise it, feel it and receive it. Remember every action of giving thanks will automatically cause its opposite reaction of receiving so GIVE ALL TO RECEIVE ALL!

You can find a wonderful Guru or teacher and practise Yoga, Meditation, Kriya and Pranayama to release blocked negative emotions from your body and guide you on your path towards Self-Realisation. Go to bed early and get enough beautifying, repairing sleep for your soul to rejuvenate. Before sleep go into meditation where you feel good and feel true gratitude for your blessings and challenges, as this makes space for abundance! FINALLY, LOVE YOURSELF AS SELF-LOVE IS THE MAGNET THAT ATTRACTS SOUL MATES, PERFECT HEALTH, PROSPERITY AND ALL THINGS TO YOU!

BIBLIOGRAPHY

1. Yogiraj Gurunath Siddhanath: 'Winge to Freedom', Alight Publications, Page 24
2. Buddha Quote: Page 28
3. Paramahansa Yogananda: 'Autobiography of a Yogi', Self Realisation Fellowship, Page 29
4. Dalai Lama Quote: Page 51
5. Yogiraj Gurunath Siddhanath: 'Wings to Freedom', Alight Publications, Page 64
6. Sogyal Rinpoche: 'Glimpse After Glimpse', Harper One, Page 103
7. Emmanuel's Book 2: 'The Choice for Love', Bantam Books, Page 106
8. Kahil Gibran: 'The Prophet', Heinemenn: London, Page 109
9. Buddha Quote: Page 119
10. Martha M. Christy "Your Own Perfect Medicine" Wishland Inc Page 139
11. Jesus: 'King James Bible', Luke 6:38, Page 142
12. Eckhart Tolle: 'A New Earth', Penguin Books, Page 158
13. Christine Northrup MD: 'Women's Bodies, Women's Wisdom', Bantam Books, Page 160
14. Louise Hay: 'You Can Heal Your Life', Hay House Publications, Page 160

15. Abraham Hicks: 'Ask and it is Given', Hay House Publications, Page 165
16. Maharishi Mahesh Yogi: 'Science of Being and the Art of Living', International SRM Publications, Page 177
17. Dalai Lama Quote: Page 196
18. Albert Einstien Quote: Page 178
19. Nelson Mandella Quote:Page 202
20. Doreen Virtue "Angel Tarot Cards", Hay House Publication: Page 232
21. Ösho: Philosphia Perennis Vol 1; Osho Books, Page 240
22. Neale Donald Walsch: 'Conversations with God', Movie, Page 244
23. Napoleon Hill: 'Think and Grow Rich', Mind Power Press, Page 260
24. Jesus Quote: 'Bible', Luke 17.22, Page 262
25. Abraham-Hicks: 'Money and the Law of Attraction', Hay, House Publications, Page 276
26. Mariane Williamson Quote: Page 277

Joanne Lee Philpot
www.divinelifeyoga.co.uk

Sat GuruYogiraj Siddhanath
www.siddhanath.org

The Divine Babaji